T0066851

My Personal Stop Message

BeBop

Order this book online at www.trafford.com
or email orders@trafford.com

Most Trafford titles are also available at major online book retailers.

Printed in the United States of America.

ISBN: 978-1-4907-2149-1 (sc)
ISBN: 978-1-4907-2150-7 (e)

Trafford rev. 02/13/2014

North America & international
toll-free: 1 888 232 4444 (USA & Canada)
fax: 812 355 4082

PREFERENCE

It is recommended you do not even touch this kind of truth about life on the down side if you are the ole' fashion, with its philosophy thinking, very religious individual living with the rest on these lands. It is believed this may be too much for you to try and endure. If indeed you are strong enough in whatever faith you live and you seek to know the thinking pattern and life style of the many suffering the negatives of life then by all means endure this one depiction of a gay, black brotha in what is much of a diary kind of format. It will allow you the truth about life lived by just one unique individual among the many under the guidelines of the negative life so many live. This one life gives reference to many other lives encountered in the same wilderness and the suffering that gets so involved and intense. Be aware that what you are about to endure is a true encounter of only one individual having made it to hopeful safe grounds after the storm; that we as humans make mistakes on levels many would think could never happen. And for you who may be looking for a story of life similar to your own this may be what you seek; especially if you may be thinking of taking your own dirty laundry to the wash house. Many in this category could use some real inspiration to help make that one final and as well real decision to make that change. The truth about making that turnaround a reality will hopefully be endured in this story. For educators, doctors and others wanting more of the scope or picture of life in such a negative world and its thinking process as well, this story may pinpoint a more complete and overall view thus giving those in the mental, medical, counseling and other related fields a better focus on dealing more successfully in this area of life. It is especially noted in this story how those in the study field could maybe look more deeply into the desire for change and how so many years of such a pattern of life has its effects on making such a change. It is known how there continues to be the successful work to date in this area taken from expressed and open such stories and its experiences and I am sure more unique experiences are wanted in this area of study. Pay particular attention to the education sought allowing for depiction of the negatives and even positives in life that lead to decision making. There is included the kind of poetry of a brief and new era nature hopefully allowing for the kind of better understanding in all levels of academics in our total society. For the one looking for entertainment this just may get you some satisfaction but may leave you with questions if indeed you make it all the way through without the excitement turning into the boredom of not really finding the continuous nasty plot sought after. This continues to be my way of making sure I stay alert and on top of a new world free of the past—a past I term "Yesterday". This true depiction of life may indeed baffled or get one caught up in the kind of understanding that I believe need the true empathy of one enduring such an account before, during and after the "high". Make note how this can be a kind of autobiography as there is expression and its depiction of my childhood, life growing up, my lost youth and the ramifications into today after "yesterday". Expressing the period from prison to the time of finding true recovery is done in the order that it follows. The ongoing diction or my diary are the thoughts and actions taken from the point of my last ever "hit" of and desire for drugs of any kind including nicotine. From this point after the 'hi' are what is referred at as 'Back To Writings" or the hard work encountered to date. These are personal expressions or entries into my diary to come after enduring what I believe is the preparation done up to such a point.

My Stop Message

*If more under the power and insanity of addiction could
stop long enough to focus on beginning of a fresh new
day without the plague of a bottle of wine, a balloon,
spoon and its outfit, a hit and its accompanying glass
pipe or anything that must be ingested in some way
to relieve the pressure and pain felt by addiction.*

*If such could stop long enough to watch the sun rise and
endure its soothing warmth and tremendous energy instead
of what has become a pest in the sky burning and getting in
the way of another beautiful day that can never be seen.*

*Stop and try to remember what your teeth were like before
this monster called addiction took over the direction of your
hygiene. Remember what your bathroom was like around this
same time and if you showered or bathed on a regular basis.*

Stop long enough to hear an ole jam mastered by one of the greatest of strings being played on a distant radio. Remember those days and how life was indeed BREEZIN'.

Stop and reflect on the last night's peaceful and most comfortable slumber. As well reflect on that significant other you cherish to this day and how the two of you awoke to that beautiful dawn. And in such waking, after experiencing a night never to forget, the two of you put a seal on your love aided even more by the dawn and its rising sun.

Recall if you will the times on a regular basis when breakfast, lunch and dinner were hot and tasty meals. Remember if such was the reason for all those diets. Remember the service you were treated with at the local supermarket due to the checks that were always honored because not one of them ever bounced.

Recall, if you will, how your identification to verify checks had been replaced by your wide smile.

Compare your domestic quality today to yesterday. I mean; when was the last time you were complimented for your domestication for a bright and cheerful home?

Stop and calculate the last most consistent lot of paid: rent, gas, electric, newspaper, ebony, jet, playboy, phone, internet and cable bills—not to forget house notes for those of you. And by consistent I refer to that lot of paid bills years old now. And while you're calculating find those receipts for that wide screen television set with DVR, that stereo system with its thousand plus collection of your favorite

music, that gold watch with the diamond midnight mount,
other jewelry shared out of love and the late model car.

Pause for moment to think about how peaceful, even with
all the bull, life was compared to the mad insanity that is
found to only fix that never ending problem of today.
Maybe after just some of this reflecting one may begin
to do more wanting, desiring and yearning other than
those times we can get backed up against a wall. As long
as that need does not arise those of us who keep saying,
"hey; maybe I need to", may have a shot at recalling
to light that missing sun and all its fresh glory.

You may even find that a rainy day has certain
freshness to it for all its intended purposes.

Like the rain after some polluted problem in a downtown or
ghetto alley you think of that monster you are polluted by as
the very same. And a good hard rain can be thought of as those
tears and flow of snot all pouring without the thought of a
man crying or a woman giving in both to surrender. And like
the rain there is something fresh and clean throughout that is
seen and felt as strength, courage and especially humbleness.

On the first sun shinny day after the cleansing rain can
be seen and felt the very same intensity after one's own
shower—OH YES! It's alright to cry! At least for me it
was and is still today. As well there are those I walk with
in this fresh new world who feel the very same. There are
those witnessed on a regular basis who feel the beginning
of this brand new world free of the chains of insanity.

And if pride should stand in the way of so much pain suffered by addiction than it is only my suggestion that maybe you wait for one of Seattle's many rainy days or New York, Chicago or Atlanta's many buckets of rain and walk in it. No one except our Higher Power will notice you in the midst of a wet crowded downtown or lonely ghetto street CLEANING HOUSE . . .

BeBop

I

From Prison To San Francisco

October weather is a cooling period from the always beautiful summers in Washington State. In October 1986 I was released from the Reformatory in Washington State after serving a second term. Doing time in this state ain't no joke. A seven and a half year mandatory sentence indicates one will bring five years three months before consideration of parole. A five year mandatory sentence is about three years four months of this straight time before one is considered for parole. No wonder college and general education (GED) along with social interaction with outside organizations are encouraged. After the second term in the reformatory and a year after found at home in Seattle accomplishing nothing with the two associate degrees and GED earned in prison I felt it was time to leave my home given the first possible chance. Add to this having experienced for the first time in my life the ridiculous out-of-the experience called tweek from smoking crack cocaine. During this period family members and friends and what I will call personal

1

encounters had all smoked or engaged in drugs and alcohol with me. But with crack at that time I could not get the mad rush or effects of a 'hella-high'. Instead it was better to shoot the powder form of cocaine and get a rush out of this world. Seems almost all of my immediate longtime friends or better termed 'potnas' were all experiencing crack with sexual overtones—a luring factor used to enhance the so called beauty or intensity of the high. And that seemed to work for me only temporarily because the first sexual encounter after having smoked crack and shooting powder cocaine found me waking the next day to my cocaine and money stolen. Thus a new life in a bigger city looked, tasted, felt and altogether seemed more and more the adventure that was soon to come. After all at almost 38 years old I had hardly been anywhere in my adult life except prison. Had I got away about two decades earlier maybe the talent for art would be a big plus in my life today. Maybe I could have gone to school to enhance and learn the ropes of being an artist and make a career of a hobby I truly have much love and interest in instead of being the 'self-taught' artist that is a part of my vitae. But, like a wonderful full of love voice loved since childhood I'm not going to focus too much on yesterday's as I too believe so much in such memories. Thus I left after over a year out of prison having worked and achieved the status of an altogether free man whose debts to society were paid and travel outside the scope of parole a choice completely my own. I was now free of active parole and would be off parole totally after a number of months from any trouble with the law—which I became free of. I could now relocate in any state and the many cities in the country. Assessing any possibility of addiction to cocaine or its crack form did not occur at all after the decision became clear in my mind to relocate and as well where to find new excitement in my life. After all the previous adventure with drugs from pot, psychedelics, speed, downers, not to forget the cheap fortified wine known as Thunderchicken; nothing had grabbed me by the neck and choked me more than crack cocaine. I may very well have escaped a life of drugs if not for this awesome form of addiction found in my generation that kept me in constant search for something new—a natural feeling that did not mature as it normally should have. Maybe all the drugs experienced yesterday and how I thought I was never really addicted to such was a setup for what crack cocaine came along and did to my life after leaving my home in Seattle due to, as mentioned, the crack cocaine high not being what it was to everybody else. Work was never too much of a problem as I did not mind it knowing the importance of security. Little did I know that this priority had begun losing its value due to having spent almost all available monies from work and saving prior to finally departing my home in Seattle while on the initial crack cocaine experience. Being furious over the loss of money and dope due to theft really had no violent effect on me except for the thoughts of revenge that were overpowered by the desire to leave my home that much sooner. Add to this an experience in art and a sexual gay affair that I held off and on for almost two decades helping me to make the decision to leave. I remember paroling for the second of three times. I got busy with a job and obtained my own apartment in Seattle's Capitol Hill area. I also hooked right back up with my Texan, Jay E, after nearly four years away from him as was done the first time paroling from the Reformatory. There was also the intense desire to get to work with my world in art found the very first day in a prison cell as I had even more practice and a desire to put as many of the wonderful music legends on canvas as my ability would allow. The world of music is an infinite one. A very intense experience is recalled the day I obtained a canvas and art supplies, some weed, some alcohol and the company of Jay E. This I thought was the kind of atmosphere and setup wanted to ultimately venture into and create even better versions or portrayals of the music legends on canvas I had created in prison. I recall this day getting all set to put another of many favorite jazz legends I am very fond of on canvas. This canvas I thought would be the beginning of my getting into my work outside of prison. During parole the first time out of prison I never touched or so much as thought about my love for art and what I wanted to create in it. But it was found how the new kind of atmosphere that included chemical addiction— something new to creating art—and Jay E's addiction and attitude to go along with it all turned out a canvas that had no depth, no highlight, no perception or likeness nor any of the personality in my world of art I had been so blessed to discover the first day in prison. The portrait seemed to favor a stick-man version of Popeye the Sailor man. This caused greater frustration in my life with the horrible feeling of failure. Thus came the decision to gather whatever funds and materials available and go with the choice made to head for San Francisco and make my home there. San Francisco was the choice that found me buying a one way Greyhound ticket in the very early morning of December 6th, 1986 around 1:30am. I boarded that greyhound bus headed for the gay capitol of the world. After all I am also a so-called 'sexual deviant', having experienced many homosexual encounters during my life— especially the sixteen years spent with my first lover and the ten years in prison. Living among so many free minded people of all kinds as expressed to me by those visitors of that city I felt putting my life together in San Francisco would be a real easy task. But I must remind you that I have never ventured outside my home in Seattle except for the ten years spent in that state's prison system and overnight and weekend trips to Canada and Portland, Oregon. I had become a follower attached to such as prison's institutionalization and the continued battle I had with my family especially concerning my sexuality. On this morning of my departure from what was really a home I love dearly was my very best and dearest 'potna' RJ. RJ full of crack and vodka shed many tears at the greyhound bus station. I'll never forget the look on his face. Thinking about the times we shared together from my teenage years into adulthood saw more good times than any bad. The one thing I didn't take into consideration was how much joy I brought into his lonely life, especially after my having reached adulthood. All the people I knew from childhood to prison as well as an alcoholic speed-freak mother for him to drink with all made his life pretty happy. RJ is from the east coast and not so young anymore. I would say he is between me and my mother's ages which would make him just about 53, at the time of this writing, if indeed he was born in 1938. His birthday I can never forget as it is 26 days before mine in the same month. In fact two birthdays back home outside my family's I can never forget are RJ's, March 2ⁿᵈ and Tilly's, April 24ᵗʰ. Tilly as well made great friends with my mother some years prior to my leaving letting me know mother had finally excepted my life as a gay man and its life style as well as the good friends I carefully chose. Tilly was a source for me to hang out when I ran away from home during younger teenage years. I would clean his apartment while the older adult gays drank and played pinochle—a part of me I did not know Mother had instilled in me so very well. Tilly was a professional chef at one of Seattle's five star hotels but not so good at keeping a bright and cheerful home. Tilly was far from domesticated in this area. But he could cook up a batch of ox tails that you just could not keep your fingers off of. Tilly saw where my domestication came from after seeing mom's home just three blocks down the street. Not just anyone could get to be friends or develop a relationship with Tilly or RJ. It took more methods of attention and years than I care to count or think about to reach their hearts and confidence. But I had to give these wonderful friends up. RJ, my very best potna, left me with an emotional image full of tears that traveled many miles down the west coast. I remember so well how RJ accepted me bit by bit over a decade of time. After I was finally a young adult and trying to become as independent as possible from mom—which was so hard to do—he, RJ, was my first roommate. I had shacked with a girl I grew up with before this. We were childhood sweethearts and I still believed we actually loved each other. Little did we know that our private lives were intruding on each other's happiness. I'll always love you Lee Lee—you ole Dyke. RJ was and still is, in my heart, the father image I never shared with a beloved older person, not even as much as certain family members I had clung to. Tilly and RJ passed away in the 1980's. My life with drugs before crack cocaine rarely got involved with the actual using a lot of drugs. Downers, speed and alcohol were the big thing back then when RJ and I had lots of fun. But I chose to sell more than anything. Guess if there was a drug I took more back than it was the downers and the cheap 'Thunderchicken' wine mentioned earlier. I met, fell in love with for the first time in my gay life at twenty years old and matured a sixteen year relationship with a Texan who I believed made my life happy. RJ and I were roommates for a few years before the separation of my Texan, whatever kind of life I lived and my family in Seattle found me in prison for the first time. Don't forget even though elaboration will not get into deep expression of my younger years; I did mention a rearing in the drug scene apart of any ghetto. Thus a saint I was not and in fact was very far from. If you want to hear or find out about my sexuality and my raising I expect your responses will let it be known after encountering this part of my life addicted to crack. I am thinking this personal part of my life will probably interest the many addicted lives that smoke the most astounding, most awesome and most devastating drug to come along and claim such victory with its popularity—crack cocaine! The journey through my younger adulthood and those teenage years were not filled with the cold notion of using drugs, carrying a gun and obsessed with the fast life that is so apart of the norm turned out on gangs and violence of today's crack cocaine youth—of which there are as many as were the pot smokers in my times of the 1960s. My life had other meaning. But in the ghetto with a closet door to worry about among so many other things I fell into a list of traps rather willingly. Such kept me an innocent victim of homosexuality and being a dibbler and dabbler with drugs. But all this did not stop me from growing and finding RJ, Tilly, my Texan and now the cold blooded low life of San Francisco's downtown area called the Tenderloin full of crack cocaine—a trap in any big city's downtown core. I even love RJ and Tilly more than my own uncles—one located in San Francisco. He, Uncle Luc, is a big-shot in the merchant seamen's profession. When my brotha was fourteen my uncle came along and gave him an opportunity at being a seaman. I just cannot seem to recall his ever offering me the opportunity although Uncle Luc may have wanted me to wait for the sixteen months that separated me and brotha's ages. Gathering together all available cash and materials did not amont to much at all except for the dozen or more canvases I had created in prison. A little over a hundred dollars and an overnight bag that included some undergarments, few cosmetics, my GED and both associates all made travel pretty easy. After purchasing a ticket to San Francisco there was not even enough to get a cheap hotel room for the first night upon arriving in the city by the bay. In fact I ate most of the thirty bucks up during the more than twenty hours bus ride to the bay area. This led to the first experience so apart of a drug and or alcoholic's life—homeless shelters. I never knew of such emergency housing or homelessness back home. The bus station was located in the vicinity of the Tenderloin. The shelter I stayed in was not very hard to find. The flow of the environment alone was enough to let one's nose sort of lead the way to the mainstream or core of the city's function in the Tenderloin. Asking around found this day center for homeless people and a signup list for shelter the first night in San Francisco. It was already night upon arriving and around eleven PM I was at the Anaram center just in time to cop a spot on a mat on the floor of this emergency shelter. The next day was certainly a busy day for me after having thought about the steps to take to survive and come up from such a bottom. These thoughts included how much better than this I was. What I, again, had not realized is how I was into the very initial stages of addiction and would soon be accepting this way of life with its missions and street life without reservation. After the experience of a mission I decided to get in contact with Uncle Luc. After all it had been some years since seeing him. I wanted to see if he was still the mean looking businessman I had depicted him to be since childhood. Upon locating him a few days into the city I found that even though he was not the most cheerful fella he did give me a hundred dollars and got me situated in a hotel where crack cocaine filtered its permanent sting into my life. After seeing my uncle that one time and my brotha that Christmas, 1997, I never saw them or tried to contact them again. Crack needed all possible attention. As mentioned I knew the value of working—a value I had not lost in the very early stages of addiction, but had begun to suffer maintaining. In fact at this stage I could never admit being addicted because I honestly did not know what addiction was. My value for work had kept me working in a company worked for since Seattle of which was transferred to the San Francisco location. This was a good move on my part as I thought I needed and wanted to relocate away from home. Work began in this telemarketing outfit within a few days after arriving in the bay area. Time continued on and paychecks earned began the start of a nightmare that continued over a period of more than three years which included several other jobs, welfare checks, food stamps and whatever else that got me the satisfaction of that damn hit of crack cocaine. The telemarketing job consisted of selling a line of products for a notable company. The hottest selling item in this outfit was a line of five year guaranteed light bulbs. In Seattle I had learned the basic selling pitch and had developed my personality and confidence for selling these products over the phone—the medium used to sell these products. I was and can still be a telemarketer. This career may have been just that except loneliness got in the way of work and ease of mind. I needed friends, sex, love and those innocent things any human being craves. At this job are handicap people of all kinds as the company hires only those with some handicap who can handle the business of selling their products. Having a handicap also includes "having been" addicted. My epilepsy and a rising addiction to crack allowed me immediate status of employment in this company. My ability to sell continually increased. One big problem stayed apart of this nationwide organization—those addicted handicaps still actively using. This was a bigger problem than actually known when I worked there and is probably still just as bad if not a growing problem in this company. In Seattle I met several workers in the company who either smoked, shot or snorted cocaine. Our encounter never materialized due to my short stay of just over a year and my growing desires to leave my home which finally came to light fourteen months after parole from the reformatory. Add to this my devotion to family as well as my close relationships with RJ, Tilly and my Texan, Jay E. There were just not enough days in the week or weeks in the month to develop the relationship I already had established during my employment. Although time to get to know each other was limited I did manage to cash my checks at the same check-cashing spot. On many occasions back then I was given the ole "know where I can cop" line that almost began what would have been the start of many days and nights together wrapped up in the experience of cocaine. I could have very well become totally addicted back then, but the challenge to conquer more than my home in Seattle plagued me so very intensely. This reason kept me from using a lot of drugs with family and friends at home due to my wanting to be as good an ex-convict as possible in hope of early parole, which as mentioned did in fact happen and is what gave me the opportunity to depart my beloved home in Seattle. What laid ahead for me would come soon enough.

WHAT LEVEL OF LIFE IS THOUGHT OF?

TO OBSERVE HUNDREDS OF HUMAN LIVES ON THE
FLOORS AND DONATED JAIL BUNKS, LYING SIDE BY
SIDE, TRYING THEIR BEST TO END ANOTHER DAY?

TO FIND IT IS AGAIN TIME TO RISE WITH THE
MANY BIRDS, WHO HAVE ACHIEVED A MUCH
CLOSER RELATIONSHIP WITH MAN ESPECIALLY AT
THIS LEVEL, TO BEGIN ANOTHER DAY WITHOUT
A CHANCE TO CLEANSE AND FEED THE BODY?

TO FIND THE MATS SLEPT ON IN THIS BARN-LIKE
DORM STACKED IN SEVERAL LARGE PILES WITH
JUST THE SWEEPING OF ITS FLOORS THAT WILL
OPEN UP ANOTHER 24-HOUR DISEASED VENTURE?

TO FIND ANOTHER CHURCH COMING
'ROUND TO FEED WHAT IS GENERALLY
THE ONLY REAL MEAL OF THE DAY?

TO FIND IT IS SO MUCH EASIER TO RELIEVE THE
MIND, BODY AND SOUL OF THIS SUFFERING WITH
ADDICTIVE CHEMICALS—BE THEY WET OR DRY?

TO FIND HOW IT IS THIS NORM HAS ACTUALLY
BECOME ADDICTED TO THIS ATMOSPHERE
AND OVER TIME HAS BECOME A SOCIETY?

*TO FIND THIS SOCIETY A DEFINATE PART
OF HUMAN LIFE WHERE EACH GROUP OF
SUFFERERS: GAYS, GANGSTERS, ADDICTS,
DYSFUNCTIONAL FAMILIES, MENTAL DISABILITIES
AND OTHERS IN SUCH LIFE HAVE LEARNED
NOT TO LIVE WITH EACH OTHER BUT INSTEAD
HAVE LEARNED TO SUFFER TOGETHER?*

*TO FEEL THE VIBES AMONG SUCH SUFFERING
THROUGH A FIGHT IN THE FEEDING LINE
BETWEEN A GAY AND A GANGSTER?*

*TO KNOW HATRED, WITH ITS VIOLENCE, MAKE
IT AN EVEN HARDER TASK FOR THE WORK OF
GOD, THORUGH HIS CHURCHES, TO EXTEND
WHAT SEEMS TO BE THE ONLY REAL HELP?*

*TO SEE AND KNOW HOW IT IS SATAN HAS
INDEED INVADED THIS ENVIRONMENT OF
HUMAN LIFE CONTROLLED BY HIS DRUG
SELLING GANGSTERS, MENTAL DISABILITIES,
DISTORTED AND ABUSED BEHAVIORS, HATE,
VIOLENCE AND OTHER NEGATIVES MAKING
UP THE HELL SATAN THRIVES ON?*

II

The Beginning Of Addiction And New Friends

Having departed my home, tasted the preliminary experience of what had become the most popular drug of choice in America, transferring the position held as a telemarketer in Seattle to the San Francisco location and getting initially settled with a place to stay; the stage was now set for the incorporation of crack cocaine into my life. Time is a very important element in our lives. When time seems to be going by too fast may be because it is aided by some unwanted ultimate end exampled by being unprepared for final exams or there is not enough time to continue enjoying something exciting and fulfilling—"the party is over y'all". To the contrary when time seems to go by very slow where a hour feels like a whole day and nights are sleepless where two nights seem packed into one tend to be caused by loneliness, nervous anticipation, worry and the like—end of a love affair. After arriving and becoming situated the first few days in San Francisco I was unaware of a process that had already begun that called for social and personal satisfaction with its interaction. Having experienced sleeping in an emergency shelter, better known as a mission, sharing the floor with mats to lay on among many other homeless individuals with many in and around my age; I began realizing the need for social interaction, sex, friends and their good old friendly conversation, a joint of weed or a drink with someone and maybe a game of spades or better yet a game of pinochle with a possible date thereafter—a date with the looser of course. Having taken care of much business over the initial days on the bay with the finding of the telemarketing company and getting right back to work selling those same light bulbs and cleaning products, getting a place to stay and a little money for food and such, thanks to Uncle Luc, and getting to know my way around the area I lived in on ninth and Mission I felt the urges especially for sex. Thinking about the faces, some sad and many happy, in this social mix at the mission grew very strong very quickly over a period of a couple days. At work? You know from the expression of the kind of work and the people selling over the phone what kind of temptation I found myself attracted to. The money Uncle Luc had furnished me delayed any immediate return to the day centers of the missions located in and around the Tenderloin. The start of telemarketing on Market Street in the area of the Tenderloin found the thirst for my interaction with others quickly quenched. As mention, telemarketing became an even better trade for me than had been at home. I began making sells and becoming even more comfortable with the selling pitch the first day on the job. To reflect back on making friends found how long and complicated a task it was to become friends with RJ and Tilly back home. Would I have to do this again? The process of getting to know and develop enough confidence before opening up a heart full of welcome came quickly even though I had to make that first move on the job with fellow workers—a trap totally unaware of. With the fifty or so bucks left from the money Uncle Luc had been kind enough to give me was the perfect opportunity to invite or lure the company of someone I had my eye on for the last three days of work at this new job, in this new environment, many miles away from home, feeling free as the jail bird I now was. It was the third evening after work I ask Reggie if I could buy him a drink. He began his acceptance speech with how well I was doing on the job and if I was from the bay area and his being raised in the city. Comfort sat in almost immediately. Dude was in his early thirties although he lied about his age saying he was 39 maybe due to my revealing my being 38 years old. Don't really know if there is any real psychological connection or value that warranted his wanting to be superior to me in order to dominate the relationship that began that very night. This very night after the introductory conversation between us saw how a drink was not the main item on the menu that we both wanted. His asking if "I smoked" was responded to with a positive answer by my asking where I could cop a ten dollar bag of bud (marijuana). This was not the smoke Reggie had in mind and ask if I had ever smoked 'Rocks'. This new language I found needed my undivided attention. I had learned from Reggie that rocks were a class of cocaine. After expressing my initial experience with it including how these rocks had not had the effect others raved about I could see I had made what was to become a brand new friend—a great friend! Instead I was simply a choice "duck" with a job and even a couple of twenty dollar rocks in my pocket in cash form. This began the relationship. Off we went to Turk Street to find his connection. From there, with not one or two but three twenty dollar rocks, it was off to my hotel on ninth and mission. On this evening with Reggie, the commander of operations, I experienced what was from that night on to be the worst addiction ever to any drug including alcohol in my entire life. Reggie had with him a glass pipe already prepared with the screen known as brillo or copper wire inserted in the bowl of the glass pipe. He cut the first rock with a single edge razor blade into one piece hits and inserted one in the pipe. He then instructed me on how to draw the white smoke from the pipe, similar to hitting a joint of pot. He held the flame from a bic lighter for me as I had no knowledge of melting the rock and creating this white smoke—the white fog full of the cocaine in its based form that created the rush I experienced for the first time in my life. After inhaling this smoke and holding it for approximately ten seconds Reggie instructed me to release this fog in my lungs and ask me how I felt. A total insane and crazy madness came over me. Sex instantly entered my mind causing an erection never felt with any other drug or even sober as in being in prison for a long period of time sex-abstinent. Reggie let it be known that being in San Francisco would find me every kind of sex I ever dreamed of especially that of homosexuality as he is gay—something I was not sure of until this night experiencing the high that was fast becoming so popular especially among my Black culture. I was only just another brotha being initiated with honors into the awesome addiction of crack cocaine. Paranoia was found to be the major characteristic of the crack cocaine high. With this sexual devastation along with Reggie's open statement of his sexuality together with the fear of my being kicked out of a closet I chose to hide my own sexuality in came instant paranoia. It has never been my desire to flaunt my sexuality though I did in my earlier gay and younger years—teenage and twenties. I thought I was more of a bi-sexual man due to ever present desires for the opposite sex. Keeping my sex life pretty much a part of my private life allowed me complete satisfaction of sexual desires unlike those who actively and openly live a flaming gay life. I chose those socialites who live and yearn for basically the same sexual desires or who prefer to mix with those of my bi-sexuality who too do not care for the flaming glamor such as cross dressing and the like. Reggie is of such caliber but again the shock of his open statement in the privacy we shared and the initial rush of crack cocaine sent me into immediate paranoia. This syndrome, a part of the crack high, is very contagious and became the highlight of the remaining evening and early AM hours. The crack had been smoked as well as the remaining twenty dollars left from the first purchase of rocks. There are other symptoms associated with the paranoia of the crack high. Intense paranoia brings about the fear of someone listening in on your conversation. Thus in a hotel there is peaking out the entrance door's peep hole, listening with ear to the hotel room door, looking or peering from the side out the window and always thinking the police are coming any second. Add to this an even more peculiar behavior caused by the crack high that keeps one's fingers in constant search for a crumb or pebble of crack thought to be dropped during the smoking process. This occurs near or at the end of the supply of crack and money to buy more. It is believed that the fear of not being able to continue the high creates this out-of-the-norm behavior. It would take the knowledge of those educated minds to explain these strange behaviors in their scientific format. But this is an evaluation, of sorts, from a very recent continuous user's point of view. The rush felt after each hit lasts only a few minutes at the very most. This causes the pattern which leads into hit after hit in pursuit of the rush felt with each piece of crack melted and smoked through a crack pipe. After coming down from each hit there lies an uncontrollable urge to again achieve the feeling of the last hit which is why any supply will deplete in a very short time also causing all money and material value to be depleted in pursuit of purchasing more crack to fulfill the urge for this craved rush. The experience I had with Reggie ended in his departure later that night. But sex with him ended up in masturbation because paranoia had set in so intensely that enjoying sex between the two of us could not be fulfilled. I was somewhat surprised that ejaculation from the two of us masturbating was a success. It brought the paranoia down a great deal and enabled us to continue what was to be a relationship that carried on for over a year. This kind of time as friends found many days smoking, 'tweeking' and 'geeking' along with pursuing the many 'missions' for more and even more crack cocaine an endless journey. I met dealers, visited crack houses in the Fillmore, Valencia Garden and many other places as well as the main den of sin—the Tenderloin. Smoking crack everyday cannot happen unless the supply is somehow limitless through being successful at dealing and still being able to smoke to satisfy such a huge continuous lust or resulting to living in the streets selling sex and pulling robberies or whatever else it would take to survive from day to day with this huge thirst for crack. In my situation, like so many, it was the continuous weekly cycle of paychecks earned at the telemarketing gig. During the first few months it was pretty easy to pay the 65 bucks a week for rent and smoke the rest. Can it be imaged what kind of living conditions I lived in for this kind of money—in the Tenderloin at that? When the money ran out usually that night or the next day and sex was finally accomplished, if at all, there was a cooling off period experienced many times alone and sleep would allow the intense craving to subside. Thus I was not the mad and raged addict so many are plagued by causing every day to be the ultimate crack cocaine of their lives. Instead the next day would begin, for me, a hard working cycle for the next week's pay in order to do it all over again. This brings to mind a period where I was so frustrated because of this cycle of endlessness until one night over a year down the rocky road I began pondering quitting this awesome drug. My solitude began a pattern of writing about what I had obviously found myself trapped in—a vague but sure beginning of admitting my helplessness and addiction to crack. This was during a time Reggie and I had parted for a short period of time due to his being a hustler compared to my being a working man. The two lifestyles involved in the same trap of crack could not mix with consistency. Reggie stole money, crack and even lured other sex partners from me after having smoked all my money up. In such solitude of shame, guilt, hatred and especially pity for myself, I came to realized one thing I was still pretty good at even without a four year college degree—a bachelors still holding faith to achieve one day. Writing began basically with what I call crack rap. One night in October, 1988 in my solitude began a 22 volume package of crack rap. I wrote crack poems straight from an addicted and craving mind. But during the remaining two years of missions, jobs, prison and all that ended up in despair over my continued use, I lost all but one crack poem which was the only one embedded into immediate memory. All the other spoken word poems such as: Hayday on Payday, Rumors, From Turk to Mission and many more were no longer remembered and therefore could not remain in memory as did the "The Effects of the Blast":

DO YOU KNOW WHY ONE GOOD BLAST WON'T LAST? YO' SUCKA; IT COULD BE THE PYCHOLOGY MASTERING YO' IMMEDIATE PAST.

YA' SEE; AFTA ONE GOOD HIT;
YA' THROW DOWN WIT;
AAHHH SHIT! CAN I GET ANOTHER LITTLE BIT?

NOW THIS GOES ON UNTIL THE VERY END.
WHEN IT IS THE INSANITY SAYS; "HEY
FOO'; NOW DO IT ALL OVA AGAIN"!

NOW CAN YA' MAYBE SEE THE PSYCHOLOGICAL
PATTERN OF THE BLAST?
AND WHY AIN'T SUPPOSTA' GIVE A SUCKA
THE SATISFACTION TO LAST?

This type of creativity, thought to be good therapy, is still part of the work needed in the quest for my life. During the time prior to any real thoughts of discontinuing the use of crack there began a changing of jobs, hotels and even an uncompleted six month business course. Because Reggie had begun the infiltration of my finances once again, especially after quitting his telemarketing position, I decided it was time to give up the hotel I lived in for better living conditions. After about three months of work for the handicap outfit I found a short course in word processing that obtained better employment shortly before completion. The school was very centrally located allowing me to continue selling in the evening and attend classes in the AM and late afternoon hours. Even though I must pat myself on the back for trying to move up in my life and accomplish something positive; it is felt that the addiction, now in full force after the many weeks with Reggie, had only utilized my progressive knowledge skills having dictated to me the need to prioritize the maintenance of this addiction to crack. After almost five months at this business school, opportunity came very quickly. Grades and selling myself at this school were very positive and responsive. Not only was I ahead of the course by about a month; but, all my teachers were proud of my progress. Grades averaged over a 3.2gpa—my normal throughout past college years during both two year associates. Typing, as usual, was not my best subject but I achieved a strong 'C' grade. Guess I just cannot get that 70wpm with accuracy as a result. I believe this is from the numbness still felt in three fingers of my right hand from a burn accident. As with recovery, if I want it bad enough I will work at it every day until success is my victory. A good solid fifty with good accuracy along with the knowledge of the latest software, good math, bookkeeping, good English and the demonstrated quality and ability to advance in a good company found me interviewed by the president and his secretary of a very wealthy and well known religious based organization caring for wealthy and middle classed elderly people. To be accepted in this company beginning as a receptionist saw enormous room on the ole ladder to grow and gain much success and its material rewards. Going back to school to achieve this success was very essential for such advancement but far from my mind. Because the opportunity and achievement of the receptionist position came along before I was to graduate I did not bother taking the easy test in only one class left keeping me from graduating. My thoughts were on paychecks now and how they would be doubled and tripled from the days of selling light bulbs. I quickly removed myself from selling another light bulb, bought some work clothes and prepared myself as completely as possible for being this large corporation's receptionist. The position was in the corporate office which had lines to all its seven sites. The switchboard took some training but I was working with enough confidence and efficiency to hang in there for the time it took to learn and become comfortable in this position. Work in this company began on August 23, 1988. One of the main factors causing the destruction of such a break in my life was how convenient the crack hood was to access from work. It was easier to access than off hours living in the Tenderloin. This corporate site is located one block from Japan town on Geary Street while the Fillmore is located only three blocks from this part of town. Not having finished the business course after being so close to completion with such success, being given this break at the corporate site in their brand new corporate office and still baring the stupidity of loneliness and those other excuse-seeking cover-ups were all facts of what was to come over the next three months in this spacious and as well exciting new office filled with opportunity. From the deep pile carpet to the latest in computer, fax and copier equipment this office was indeed plush. Too bad every other Friday was payday which began, on the very first paycheck, this three month run on crack—one of several short kinds of runs I suffered. I had relocated to a hotel of much better quality. It had my own full shower and toilet. This was something found in previous and almost all Tenderloin and other ghetto hotels to be a rarity. Most hotels share nasty showers and horrible filthy toilets. But for around $450 a month I moved up in the world and further away from the

Tenderloin on Polk and Eddy to: shag carpet, a double bed, very few roaches, a front street window view and as mentioned my personal full bathroom in excellent condition. Paying rent became very important at this residence. Even though I was paid twice a month I managed very well because of the increased salary made at this new job. I was left with enough hundreds to do as I pleased— get a damn hit!! The hood located conveniently from work was the Fillmore where Reggie grew up. Having previously copped, prior to this new change of status, I knew I could again find a connection at the project site in this hood. Wearing a suit and tie, looking like the well to do office or company worker I could very well have become, found me much 'respect' and priority among the dealers each payday. Add to this the three hundred average dollars per visit spent on crack. Reggie came back in my life after a few weeks after meeting back up with him in his hood of the Fillmore one payday purchasing my usual. Man! Was I in need of an old familiar face to make me feel good—I thought! This was due to meeting others in this hood who were out to get every pebble and crumb they could and my being stupid and addicted enough to invite them to my spot. Not only that I would purchase hundreds of dollars in crack on my lunch break and even smoke a couple of hits in the restroom of this huge fancy corporate office just to see how good it was. Was I just too damn anxious for a hit? Reggie and I picked up where we left off but the reprimand he got from me let him know that previous activities would only end our 'potnaship' very quickly—as if such was indeed a reprimand. Instead of ending it this way I met another smoker at the telemarketing outfit as I kept ties with the star salesman (PV) and the manager at that time (HJ). Both were smokers and PV a gay blade of compatible quality. He introduced me to EJ a relationship that quickly grew into an immense affair. After only one payday and more hundreds in crack, the comfort of my hotel, the compatibility we shared and our addiction to crack EJ moved in with me. We had put the paranoia under control because, I believe, during the short period of knowing each other and the comfortable living conditions there was no need for the fake watch on the door and enough crack was there to keep the highlight of the relationship to crack alive. We even, on several occasions, hired toss-ups to enjoy sex with us for the low fee of a two or three-dollar hit of crack. Man! I really had the time of my life with EJ. All loneliness ceased. Worry about home in Seattle, family and friends all ceased completely—or continued to burn on the back burner. Sex, social desires and needs were satisfied to what seemed the fullest. No wonder we could wait between paydays to smoke. Not only was I working and making the big bread EJ was still working selling light bulbs at the telemarketing company. This allowed us to smoke every weekend, create credit with the dope man and party super hardy on my paydays. What a life!! Nothing could go wrong with such a wonderful setup. DAMNIT!! I forgot Reggie. He came back on the scene. He caused EJ to feel too relaxed as Reggie gave him the persuasive 'game' about his super good looks—of which EJ is very good looking as well as his having natural hustling quality and that I wouldn't mind taking care of him completely. Reggie is a poisonous snake. EJ's mind became full of Reggie's game. He first quit working and lied to get on GA (general assistance). Thus getting high only came about three or four times a month during September and October of 1988. See how the disease of addiction can be so misleading allowing persuasion to infect common sense. Tweeking and geeking with all of its paranoia began to set in due to lesser times getting high and EJ's sexuality. Dude is gay but I never knew of his true sexuality until seeing him again almost two years later. Even though I had question about his sexual behavior during our encounter I past it off as his being just a little bi. He kept his inner sexual desires for man inside and played a very affectionate 'butch' role. This in-depth role also had me wondering about his sexuality. The part of this adventure with crack may need the complete open expression of one's sexual desires. It was strange to have sex with women the way he desired. He got completely off in my presence which I thought was a show of his masculinity toward me. In fact I really don't believe a female could interest him without the company of a male third party—as this has been known to be part of my sexual desire. The male is the focus of the sexual experience when a woman is involved. Such is a horse of a gay color. It does however integrate with the addiction of crack cocaine as the two entirely different entities, sex and drugs go so hand in hand. I mentioned also that crack stimulates sexual desires but many times has paranoiac problems and accomplishing sex can often times be spoiled. It is difficult not to bring up episodes about crack into focus without the mention of sex episodes—whether gay or so called straight. The most enticing and luring attraction for the crack addict is sex. It is like a birthday present unwrapped yet. For example sex is sold for the reward of smoking crack with that one looking for sex with a one hundred dollar shot of crack in his pocket. The term Toss-Up was invented on the streets to differentiate the prostitute from the addicted crack addict willing to sexually do anything for just one hit of crack. One could have sex with a toss-up all night provided there was enough crack to "kibble" and "bit" the toss-up (issue a tiny bit of crack at a time). The toss-up is not only a female. In fact men make better toss-ups more times than women especially in San Francisco because of the extreme freaky quality that crack provokes in this city. I'm talking Black men with the ole well-endowed gifts in their jocks. Thus women and gays basically get extremely lustful for the sex of a male toss-up. Your own imagination at this point will depict anything done for a hit of crack. What a wild, cruel and crazy world. The times shared with the crack monster on my back was so sexually related until expressing what an addiction is on crack cannot hide this plain fact. So called heterosexual men insist on keeping their not so straight lives very confidential but the freakiest shows of homosexuality and obscene sex acts were so very much enjoyed by these men under the power of crack. Women seem to be innocent of being lesbians and condoned by the norm in places like the Tenderloin or probably in similar hoods like Los Angeles or New York. Men, however, must keep the fact quiet that sex with another man can get very deep especially when his tongue is found buried deep in another man's mouth. Nothing can be done to undo such a horrible act of homosexuality—a stigma so a part of the so-called norm of society. Add to this his enjoying the act of what had become lust instead of just sex; lust that can be just as freaky between heterosexual couples under the influence of crack cocaine's power. The ole closet; it hides a vast wardrobe. The involvement with Reggie became a thing of the past soon after Reggie, EJ and I had become smoked out and drunk off brandy one particular day. I nodded out for a few minutes while EJ decided to depart and obtain his GA check from his uncle's home in the Fillmore. Reggie began lusting even harder for EJ and started planning a rendezvous with him. After my having fell into slumber from the brandy and smoking crack Reggie again stole money, cocaine and even the pipe full of rez (buildup in the glass pipe from smoking). He departed only minutes after in hot pursuit of EJ. But I did not fall totally into slumber. Such is patterned after heroin's 'nod' effect when alcohol is mixed with crack. Upon Reggie's departure along with my knowledge of his thievery found me in hot pursuit of him a very few moments after his leaving my abode. Catching up with Reggie about two blocks away I became more furious not only about his stealing from me but how this low filthy faggot was trying to take EJ away from me. It was an instant reaction causing me to begin punching away on him in rage. He broke away from my insane anger and began trying to escape. I followed in chase through many blocks of the immediate area promising him his doom if he ever crossed my path again. The end result of the day caused the end of both relationships. Reggie had been victorious in achieving the company or possession of EJ that day. This goes to show just what a masterpiece I thought EJ was. EJ returned and began making immediate plans to move from my residence now on Polk Street. Because he had paid rent for that week he stayed on with me until he could move out. It was hard making room outside of the double bed to rest. The decision allowed EJ to lay in my bed but sex was completely out of the picture. We both suffered emotionally from this and as well there was no getting high together. A broken heart and wrecked emotions due to my having found myself a victim of attachment and infatuation for EJ caused my next paycheck and his departure to begin the destruction of the job and what little life I had left. The secretary, who was my supervisor, and I had begun to develop a relationship that included her husband, a preacher of a church partly owned by him. They took me to their church and introduced me to some of the members who were in school achieving degrees and prospering—as I should have done. Not only Black brothas but other brothas of all races as well aspired to me very quickly. One Asian brotha offered his personal finances to get me started with the fees needed for the application to enter the Golden Gate University. Destruction due to addiction caused crack to win over the decision to achieve success in the job held at this wonderful corporate site. The battle between the two was a very mean and heartless war. At one point after smoking up another check including not paying rent, I called Rev. Ray, my boss' husband and begged for help. I confessed to him my addiction to crack and he came to my rescue. Trying to get me to see other exciting and fresh things in life they, Barb and her husband invited me on a 'picnic' at a wonderful resort not far from the town of Carmel called Point Lobos. They have an adopted son of color from overseas whom I met. The four of us had a wonderful time together enjoying the beauty of Mother Nature. Hidden beaches, the trails full of squirrels that ate right out of human hands allowing petting without fear and wonderful scenery of water, land and its forests all indeed a memory never to forget. Add to this the ideas and prompting of my advancing in the company my supervisor had status in and the devotion rendered by both Rev. Ray and my boss to be of as much support as needed in my fight to win the awesome and scary battle against crack. They relayed important facts about myself seeing intelligence and exceptional ability that could carry me far in any career of my choice. Barb mentioned how the doors of success and opportunity were wide open for me if I wanted it bad enough. Yes; I indeed wanted it but crack wanted the opposite causing this war to become so complicated. The hopeful saviors out of the company I worked for along with their son left for parts unknown abroad. I believe they went to Sweden. That left me feeling like a drowning life with no courage to fight what seemed like huge thunderous waves back to shore. Crack cocaine won this battle and almost all succeeding battles that followed. Two battles thought to be my victory will be elaborated on later as they happened during the nightmare suffered smoking crack. The battle fought with crack initiated by the creation of crack rap in October 1988 saw defeat after defeat. A general reaction of all 'the morning after's that many users experience is tossing the scud missile (pipe) out the window, throwing it away, flushing it down the toilet or the most common one of smashing and stomping on it. All these ways were done many times after all the 'morning after's in deep concentration and emotional pain about the horrible continued use of smoking paycheck after paycheck now into thousands of hard earned dollars. This thinking pattern led to the temporary discontinued use of crack for periods of time broken by another paycheck and the "one hit won't hurt" syndrome which was actually the usual time span between smoking crack anyway. This is because, as mentioned, money was not available between paychecks causing the addiction to have to wait for paychecks. But the thinking pattern of quitting began the search for sobriety. One example of this search was the thought of going to someone for help—now that my boss and her family were gone. Hearing about the pros and cons of a church I will call Great Tide located in the Tenderloin of San Francisco inspired the possibility of help through the Rev. DX. I took the dirty pipe full of crack cocaine residue (rez) and attempted to approach Rev. DX at this church having previously heard of his desires to help those addicted lives finally seeking recovery. Anger set in even more with the suffering of my addiction after the rejection felt in trying to find the immediate help needed so desperately from this foundation. Unable to get a private consultation with Rev DX or someone of status was not encouraging. Add being counseled by workers dictating my need to want sobriety bad enough and their not addressing the emergency need to find a positive source to console, extend compassion, detox and extend such a hand of advice and possible help I believed were all needed in the most important initial stages of battle with such a devastating and cunning enemy. The individual under the power of addiction to crack is a victim not to be taken lightly. Crack is the enemy fighting and claiming the victory of each relapse which has little or no merit over the continued decision to quit or wanting to quit over the continued decisions to at least try and quit—what I've come to know as a final 100% decision. Telling me that I must make that decision to quit only increases crack's power to claim another victory during this long battle. Crack, a top agent working for Satan, has a very powerful arsenal to get that pipe, that needle, that bottle or whatever back into play with the victim. Excuse seeking is a biggie—another of Satan's valuable arsenal. All the church did was accept my 'gift' of a crack pipe to wave in church and claim having saved another from the hell of crack—thus excuse seeking. I was told to come back to their crack meeting that night which was a ten hour wait. Then I find that the church had made more in offerings because of such false testimony. I had not departed but hung around for hours confused and in the pain of addiction. What would I do in the meantime in such an emergency situation while waiting for this meeting they call 'Facts About Crack'? Should I go back to the den of sin and turn down any dope that may surely be offered me knowing some type of relief was needed what with my weakness and confusion plaguing me? As well in this den of sin I had become well known. It was thought from that day on how immediate positive counseling and help especially taking me out of the temptation of money and the drug environment may very well have done much more good than any harm—even to the point of victory over the crack commander employed by Satan. Having to be told to come back for the crack group was the perfect excuse used to continue the hell of crack: "If all they do is take the pipe and tell me to come back for a crack group and not being able to see Rev. DX or someone sensitive to my situation then to hell with quitting. I'll just stay like this!!" This statement was part of the denial used by the genius of the crack monster who usually achieves the quest of more crack to smoke for the victim assuring increased addiction. Even though I was being defeated by the powers of the crack monster I can't disregard the fact that the want and need as well as desire were becoming more and more a stronger arsenal in my favor with each fall or better known as relapse or maybe just straight up continued use causing deeper and more severe traumas with ugly outcomes that occurred. This little or no merit entity with each relapse grew. So it was that I at least tried to get back on positive. I showered, cleaned up my hotel room and prepared the same clothes worn for over a month at my job to continue working this job now so much in jeopardy due to an addiction continually gaining momentum. The rebuttal of the crack monster for my want and desire to quit arsenal caused the enemy to be successful in taking the addiction to new heights— thanks to not finding emergency relief at Great Tide and probably the biggest reason being my own stupidity. My attitude became an even harder asset for Satan's army to deal with. Do not get the desire confused with my giving up because, as mentioned, desire and need were also growing in strength for my own arsenal to faithfully emerge one day. I did in fact go to that 'Facts About Crack' meeting a few days later. In between that time I went to work and utilized the computer at my reception station to process as completely as possible the volume of crack rap I had put together in a strong attempt to say no to the poison infecting my system physically, mentally and very emotionally. The mental and emotional entities may very well have been and are today the needed factors that perpetuated the desire and want arsenal that grew in order to keep up at least a battle with Satan even though most battles were again and again lost up the end result—two battles mentioned being real challenges for Satan. After having prepared the 22 volume crack rap in print and in three ring binders I sent them to people in places of which a response never came. My get rich plan was another tactic used by Satan to keep me in denial and find me reason to give up all hope and smoke even more—excuse seeking in Satan's many forms.

Again and Again

Staff, in an invaded world of Satan's ills, continues to try and end such a situation with only the few seconds of ease they produce. Sickness still prevails on the land invaded by the devil. The few seconds or maybe minutes are depleted by the need for a clock just as equipped with the same time sickness spend on their endless journey led by Satan—24-7. The city, being aware of such sadness in a world full of yesterday's babies, are found on bikes and in patrol cars for only the time that again runs out on a clock triumphed by the negative end of life. Such a brief appearance of the city bring the hell of Satan to a brief stand-still as do staff in what seems to be headquarters for the city's homeless.

Satan holds the power of time on these stolen grounds. God watches; he knows and makes not an attempt, but instead sends a message of love through the heavy rains that wash the streets of the continued sickness, letting Satan know he cannot and will not triumph as he believes he has done. The rain, its message of love, is one of the strongest, most endured tools used by God in order to let it be known he still exists. Even though this land is clean of the sin and its degradation, there is still this ignorance that continues to find a life of pain after God's message on any street of homeless and addicted human life in America.

He sends his angels in patrol cars to help this message of love throughout the community. A few more rains keep the streets of this hell cooled and let those who continue in it know they will not be able to last for very long. After staff, the city's force and God's work the streets see little movement in the darkness at the end of another day.

Thank you God for the peace at a time when your love was needed. It is felt you will deal with a definite and final show of Satan's invasion.

III

Still In The Tenderloin More New Friends And Deeper in Debt

So called new friends and the things tried and failed finally led to what seemed the biggest failure—another several months of a crack run working for a company I say again that I should have made a real effort to become successful in. On a cold November night in 1988 only days before giving thanks I experienced what was probably a number of peaks in becoming a victim to crack cocaine. Breaking the law in order to obtain money needed for "just one more hit" was something I thought would never happen to me. But I'm an ex-convict thus . . . In the comfortable hotel I lived in there were other crack addicts I had met only recently and began smoking with. One fella, RC, had smoked with me until funds were again depleted. Craving more crack convinced us to try something I had never done throughout my so-called criminal career—snatching a purse. Being dark outside, cold and gloomy assured us even more that such an idea to obtain money this way would be a success. Off we went prospecting a victim. After only a few minutes we found an innocent looking little Asian lady walking in the well-lit busy area on Polk Street. RC pointed out how her purse was situated on her shoulder for easy snatching access and how she looked as if she had money. That was enough for me to become my own worst enemy and confirm my being Satan's slave as I busted into a gallop and swooped on this innocent victim's purse. After a few extra seconds of struggling to achieve possession of her purse I ran for anyplace safe to reap the rewards of what I thought would be my gain for such a low life show of pure and again, in another of many forms, stupidity. I found out, after all the thoughts of reaping the rewards from such a low show of stupidity, she had no money. While in the process of this criminal act there was an officer of the law not even a quarter block away. His hot pursuit and my being released from Satan's claws due to being chased by an agent of God found me in complete surrender and remorse. Never had I done something so ridiculous making me feel so utterly shameful. Having been released from Satan's ugly chains of entrapment causing an even worse feeling of fear; stopping and being apprehended by this officer of the law gave no rebuttal of any kind. Sorrow for what I had done saw tears and a relieved feeling of being caught, booked and put in jail again! During this apprehension my so called potna in crime looked on until I was handcuffed and in a police vehicle on my way to the station. To try and end the involvement with RC due to very negative feeling was found soon after the two week stay in jail, a suspended sentence and probation. He had occupied my little comfortable spot while I was in jail. Man what nerve! My stupidity or rather Satan's cue to again apply his horrible pressure effecting my peaking addiction to crack saw a few more months having encountered more smoking with RC and his potnas—end of RC! In jail for the two weeks was only a physical cleaning up period. Quilt, shame and remorse for what I had done quickly faded as the experience of San Francisco's jail saw others hooked on the negatives of life—many much worse than myself. I had accomplished something else through premeditation and planning for the very day after the short two week 'vacation' from crack. The job I had was now history except for the final pay owed to me. A quick call and a speech from the president of this company about changing my life and trying God ended in his saying he would mail my final check which arrived the same day of my release—a check in the amont of $400. Satan had been successful again. Of course these episodes are the choice highlights of so many, many scenes found tweeking and geeking on crack, getting deeper and deeper into Satan's wrath and, man, how the episodes smoking crack began to stack! It was well over a week after Thanksgiving that I was let out of jail with the $400 check. Before being released I had met a young brotha in his midtwenties in the waiting tank that holds those in jail going to court. Both KV and I received the same kick-out and probation. What does the hierarchy do with the constant flow of so many breaking the law? Turn such into an industry; who knows? Rejoicing over the kick-out and the money from my previous job began my boasting about being a free man having four hundred bucks to hunt down a hella blast with. There was no room for thinking about what the hell I was going to do to try and clean up the mess made due to the lusting addiction still and even more into full force. The ever growing nightmare I was now totally lost in could do nothing but tweek with intense craving for the first taste of satisfaction upon release aided even more by the money released with. It was easy for KV to pitch his knowledge of copping some killer crack from his uncle in Hunters Point (HP) which was like the fi nest music ever composed by Miles Davis to my ears. Off we went that afternoon to the ole check cashing spot on Market Street. From there it was a 19 Polk bus to Petrero Hill where his family lived and operated. Within an hour I had spent $150 with one of

KV's family members who had returned with three rocks of size and quality. KV and I rushed to my hotel via the same bus route where I paid another week's rent leaving me with over a hundred bucks. This is when I had to clean house of the trash that had accessed my abode having gotten in through the third floor fi re escape and my hotel window. I remember how spoiled and rotted the place seemed because of his invasion of my hotel room. But I'm a damn 'sucka' who at that time did not know just what a juicy 'mark' I was. With RC having left I voided or tried to void that past experience from my mind. A hit of crack was definitely a must. Having purchased a new scud missile and prepared this paraphernalia for a much needed blast found KV and I soon in hot pursuit of thoughts and ideas about making the kind of 'quickcash' from such a large supply of crack and still being able to smoke— the same ole sinkin'—thinkin'! Instead such a supply, of course, quickly began its usual disappearing act. That late night/ early morning was the end of all crack and money—again and indeed the usual consequences. KV's disappearance was inevitable as well leaving me in my lonely solitude. Knowing I could no longer pay rent, eat and maintain a job all opened up Satan's welcome mat and flaming doors to the hell of San Francisco's Tenderloin—his reward to me for being an excellent student majoring in pure stupidity. A day or so past the due date for the rent paid out of the $400 I packed an overnight shoulder bag, cleaned up the hotel room enabling me to get the key deposit back and became acquainted with the Tenderloin's Hostility House. This is a day center for the homeless by day and an emergency sleeping shelter for the very same at night. During the day there are cards to play— no one played pinochle—and a TV to watch. At night there are: rotten feet, unwashed bodies, cheap wine decaying many mouths, filthy clothes from coat to underwear worn continuously unwashed on these unwashed filthy bodies, mental illness and an atmosphere very detrimental to a nose fresh into this environment of homelessness. Getting accustom to such degradation was not an easy task but a task well accepted chosen over sleeping in the many doorways, park benches and living the streets filled with so many already like me—homeless and addicted. Knowledge and progressive skills were not totally damaged as the struggle for survival in this strange land called the Tenderloin became a daily part of life. I began playing cards with other homeless and addicted people hanging out for the chance at a bed each night. This facility has a lotto each night until the allotted number of beds have been filled. Getting a bed is risky business and only a few standbys after the lotto are accepted. There are no beds, cots and the like. Instead double size mats fill the facility's floor and two or three of the previously described bodies lay side by side to a mat in slumber, sickness and disease of many kinds dominated by the disease of addiction. Warehousing with its institutionalized effects were seen but never recognized at this point in my life. The struggle for survival began a search for any means and ways to come out of such degradation. Crack memories, their nightmares, good dreams, day dreams and constant thoughts turned footwork into success with the achievement of my first welfare check aside from my childhood rearing with mother having experienced years on welfare. Shortly after Christmas was the experience of the general assistance office in San Francisco. General Assistance, commonly referred to as GA, was an easy task to do in achieving the monthly $341 and some food stamps. Just be prepared to spend the day at this site among many other homeless and poverty stricken human lives. Fill out paperwork that is very simple for a high school or GED graduate but very complicated and drawn out for one with little or no education of which so many in poverty are. After a week a check is issued provided all conditions have been fulfilled. During the first day of this week I found how Great Tide church had its hands full collecting an untold amount of money per plate feeding the homeless through a government contract in the fight to keep homeless people coming back! The program of feeding the homeless consist of a meal designed to only keep starvation suppressed. Not only is there this organization but there is a catholic organization just around the corner feeding homeless as much as they can eat for approximately two hours each day. Comparing the two found me eating around the corner at the catholic foundation. It was not hard to get use to one very good meal a day. It has been my experience eating, attending the crack groups and volunteering for a very short period to hear how so many talk of the "more than seven dollars a plate or what was probably each individual's meal each day that the government pays Great Tide church for food that ends up looking like a seventy cent meal served with a teaspoon". Mind you I did not say this. I only know what I saw, heard and ate. The food is of good quality but for someone once use to eating a lot or satisfying one's hunger 'out there', there is a need for fulfillment. Add to this the need for counseling, drug and alcohol diversion, love and most of all God's understanding love instead of feeling left out, rejected, still lonely and frustrated by it all; all because one cannot say NO! It isn't as if I did not try to become part of the positive part of Great Tide church. There is such a part, isn't there? Guess I still have bad feelings from their experience. Also it is a guess that more, much more money is needed before all the love I know has to exist in this church can open up and flourish. It may be seen how disappointed I was in this church and its pastor. Sure needed a place full of love with open hands and hearts to get me on a roll to at least a beginning stage of sobriety. That ole saying about "a mind being a terrible thing to waste" fits the description of so many lost in the perils of addiction having acquired the want and desire to quit but not having enough of the fight to successfully escape; maybe due to door after impossible closed door being a nightmare even more frightening then the addiction itself. Thus; "why bother?" How surprising the number of those trapped in a world of addiction that come to this conclusion even though a better way, a clean break and the frightening nightmare of addiction are foremost on his or her minds. There are those who suffer the perils of resorting to living a homeless life on the streets in missions and the like entirely by what has become such distorted choice. I have found that these addicts console the many like me who become plagued with quality feelings, sorrow and the like during the high or peak of addiction because a sympatric ear is welcomed—very welcomed. The result is more spending until the usual end of whatever funds, however achieved with the departure of the consoling addict not so much plagued by the thoughts of this pattern of quilt and remorse—at least not yet. But this life continued on for me. GA also included a care package with meal tickets which I sold or gave away at Great Tide church. Bus tokens were also achieved along with other elements initiating me into the experience of the filthiest and most degrading rat and roach infested hotels and shelters I, a Seattleite, ever knew. The first day of application for GA was this care package. Most of the hotels are located in the Tenderloin. The Tenderloin is the more popular or central ghetto for downtown San Francisco but not the entire bay area. It is full of pornography and live nude dens, sex and related paraphernalia for sale in porno shops along with the many triple X-rated books/magazines that also make their bulk profits selling cheap wine. The tavern/pubs, small coffee and donut shops, foreign and American eateries, day centers, missions/ shelters, self-help centers and the many hotels of the worst quality help to paint this portrait of the Tenderloin. A room in any hotel is shared with hundreds of roaches and a party of rats. The toilets and showers come one to a floor. Thus all tenants on one floor share one shower and one nasty toilet—maybe two. But such is perfect for the 75 to 90 bucks a week average it will cost after the one free TL orientation week compliments of GA. Having stayed in so many of these hotels I cannot recall the first or any experience in sequential order. There were dozens of these hotels easily accessible throughout the

Tenderloin and beyond, some having several locations in the same block. Other hotels were lived in or experienced in and around the Tenderloin, some in other ghetto areas like the Mission district dominated by Mexicans and close to Valencia Gardens which is basically a black project housing unit popular for its drugs and drive by shootings. Crack infests these low level hotel hell holes condoned by the government's system of GA approved living standards for the homeless, better known during this time as 'Hotline hotels'. But the relief sought and found through GA and hotline was indeed a blessing. The invasion of crack and all the other degradation in the TL cannot be directly blamed on the governmental hierarchy. Perpetuation, though, is a contrary issue. After fulfilling the requirements for getting a GA check which include: proper identification, applying for employment benefits and fulfilling the requirements of a job search along and the most important for most seems the attendance of an orientation class which is also a contract with the government and the wealthy Rev. DX with his Great Tide church. Guess it is good this church is getting so deeply involved with the system. Hopefully more will start to occur as I haven't seen a real change in the three years of my existence in this city that warrant the possible end or tangible ease of homelessness, drugs and the like. Mind you Great Tide church may have programs similar to those offered by the norm but my view along with so many is that this church's background could very well work harder to incite more action and a coming together in such a fight for life. When people come to Rev. DX for emergency help as I did maybe he can afford then to help a victim full of crack or whatever substance with detox, emergency diversion, counseling and getting that person back on his or her feet during the emergency and it initial stages so as to maybe enable that addict/alcoholic to find help within by admitting and desiring change—a must in order to begin the relief of addiction. How does one get past the mental and emotional upset with something like crack and such without first having the physical and medical dilemmas dealt with on a real and honest level—not just the professional levels of probation, parole, jails, institutions, psychological and social therapy levels and the like that can easily make the "I don't give a damn" syndrome continue to plague the addict. I hear so much how the addict is such by choice. But so many doors are closed due to being filled to capacity or phased out of the system that the search for sobriety can easily let temptation purposely send judgment out the window and the addiction right back in for relief of those closed door replies from detox, in-house resident programs (transitional housing), rehabilitation programs and the 'how bad do you want sobriety' attitudes held by so many. No; it is not our fault, it is said, that we came to be addicted. But fighting this dilemma to victory is the addict's responsibility. Now that the addict may want sobriety there is this 'prove it' attitude caused maybe by those who use programs for temporary relief in pursuit of continued addiction, those court ordered to complete such programs and others that may tend to get nothing out of the program and get in the way of those wanting a new life free of drugs. Then I hear "if you help one out a hundred to sobriety; you've done a good job" which sounds a bit skeptical and contrary to the "prove it" attitude. Not enough faith and honest effort is given keeping a real try border lined with a mere try. A try is all the addict gives many times in return. There is always room for improvement in help programs of all types. Remember, the addict's addiction constantly searches for an excuse of any kind that will get the satisfaction of using back into play. I also hear especially in church that temptation is something we all face. When addiction gets into one's life it seems the standoffish attitude is a cover-up for one's own very possible temptation. We are all sinners . . . My experience with the Great Tide church foundation did not last long. The help I sought from the start and did not find was the beginning of a discouraging attempt at sobriety. The only asset I acquired was the awareness of my addiction to crack and the need to keep the desire to quit alive. This I believe I did. But the foundation at Great Tide was a very embarrassing experience for me when I approached them for the first time with pipe in hand and with tormented emotions as well as frightened about being addicted and gay. Before going to this house of the Lord there was a good feeling about the Rev. DX and his rescuing me with kind words and love after having made that move to seek help. Seems the thought of "make that move to seek and He will welcome thy sickness with open arms" made me feel so assuring and over enthused. His being a man of God it was my understanding Rev. DX would be that welcoming vehicle through God. On my knees I fell with pipe in hand and tears full of relief and the hurt for having fallen so low as to become addicted. But it was not the Rev. DX I saw from my knees that early morning. Instead his workers gave advice I could have used only after having been consoled and given emergency help thought to be desperately needed after almost a half year crack run. This bit of news was pretty disappointing. After thinking so positive previously I now began wondering about such a big church's sincere desire to help. Would I have to find God first in order to get my head above water long enough to be physically detoxed and mentally prepared to let a positive force in my life to fight off the ugly temptations plagued by addiction? Are there those of you thinking that if indeed I came 100% ready to change that I may have gotten the kind of welcome prescribed by our Higher Power? Not having enough knowledge of a Higher Power due to never having delved into the reality of God for myself led me to this church. The rest of the work needed in putting an arsenal together would actually be my victory if indeed I had come to the right place and come to believe. Saying no is not an easy thing to say and do when there is no one to help, guide and advise as well as give love to that suffering human being. I do know love is needed more than anything during critical times of basically any crisis. Loneliness is a negative that can and did turn high hopes of finding a positive help entity into thoughts of an impossible door to open—a usual in a city full of so many addicts. But I did manage to make it to their group and became involved somewhat in this church until an incident destroyed any existing hope after the plea for emergency help and not obtaining such. A few weeks went by and I attended a number of these 'Facts About Crack' meetings. I shared my thoughts and continued to ask for help. I offered my knowledge and whatever positives I knew I still possessed to help as a volunteer for the computer learning center at this church. I met the superintendent of the education department who left his position and the church shortly after my coming on as a volunteer. There was also a volunteer I met who was also involved in the crack group along with his lady who chaired meetings and worked in one of the church departments. He, PR, was still actively using crack and had to go in the 'closet' to continue his use due to his position and status in the church. This was something many others in the church may very well have been doing. Just before the supervisor departed the foundation at Great Tide he had set up a job for me and PR to help move a lady friend of his into the city. It took us all day and well into the night to move this lady and her roommate. The two girls moved into an apartment not far from the church. After completion and being paid sixty bucks each for the job PR ask that we be dropped off in the Fillmore on Page Street at the project site there. We had planned to pool our finances and get something big in the way of crack. Fatigue had been the perfect excuse sought after by both our addictions to plan such a party—especially with someone new and exciting. "Man; this is hard work. Sure need . . ." But before this decision to get high I had made what was only another honest attempt at quitting. I was determined to put what I felt was rejection by the church to aid the emergency need I knew should have been acted on with a positive approach aside and try this entity anyway due to the many people I felt could understand and possibly help. I was looking for positive friends and relationships needed during initial stages of sobriety. I lasted only these few weeks. It seemed like only an hour later that money and crack had again been exhausted and I was again tweeking. It seemed I had never even given abstinence a try. Finding friends at Great Tide church proved to be an experience that only got me deeper in debt. Thus it was time to try something else to escape a situation I had no confidence left in—having little from the beginning. I felt if I needed these kinds of potnas all that would be necessary was a trip back to the telemarketing job. This I did for I needed money to support a continuing habit. I found basically the same crew there. The manager, the star salesperson and I had already been smoked out on an occasion during the three month run at the ole memories on Polk Street. The position at the handicap organization lasted long enough for me to earn two checks which from that point led to GA and food stamps, homelessness, hotline/GA hotels and the like. The return to selling light bulbs ended because of the manager's successful recovery and the star salesperson's ability to maintain his status at work and the upkeep of his continuing addiction to crack. I was no longer fast enough. I found out later the manager's decision to stop smoking led him to become promoted to district manager in the company. Our negative dealings such as my borrowing money to purchase crack and the negative thoughts of each other burning constantly could not allow comfortable conditions for me to work in. The manager, HJ, took money I owed him out of my check causing an argument and my slapping the office coffee maker to the floor on my way out of that final day selling five-year guaranteed light bulbs. My final check saw the deduction for this as well. So ended the telemarketing business. From here came experiences with hotline hotels also referred to as GA hotels. Hotline hotels are achieved by the same kind of lotto method used at Hostility House where lotto tickets are issued early in the morning. The drawing is called until hotel rooms are filled that evening. The rooms are for three days whereupon the line for another hotline hotel is again necessary. This is a continuous cycle for the addict lost in addiction. Beating the system somewhat involves being on GA and acquiring a hotline hotel to escape paying rent out of the GA check. This becomes a real necessity because GA checks are completely exhausted with the crack man on check days which falls on the first and fifteenth of the month. Thus in order to possibly get a place, having exhausted the GA check, the hotline at the Otis street site, must be stood in every three days very early in the morning in hopes of making what had become known as the "lotto". If the achievement of a lotto ticket has been successful it is like money in the bank. This ticket will be cashed in at two o'clock that day and a hotline hotel again issued which has to be claimed by five PM—no later. This was done for some time. I remember the Shelta hotel during very early days on GA. There were many hotels acquired through GA and hotline. Both GA and hotline have contracts with the same hotels. Thus a GA referred hotel for one person may be hotline for the next person on the same floor next door to each other at such as the Shelta. All the experiences during this time cannot be listed in sequential order like the many hotels experienced throughout the venture in the Tenderloin. Highlights of this era and consequences as viewed today are from memory. The Shelta is a memory that depicts the earlier mention of thoughts and actions caused from smoking crack. I remember throwing the pipe out the window of this hotel after having smoked up another entire GA check. Having previously lost my overnight bag at the Hostility House due to theft, having to obtain an identification card from the GA office in order to cash the check, the cravings felt for a hit of crack all after the seven-day waiting time to achieve the check led to frustration and anger. The GA check was a relief that fulfilled the temptations and excuse seeking moves made by the addiction in me to use. Hard feelings on the 'morning-after' the disappointment as a result of my continued smoking saw the crack pipe also hurled out the widow of the Shelta. I can't even recall the so-called friends that so willingly helped me to smoke-up this GA check. There was only a day left at this hotel before the end of the seven-day GA acquired stay. The next morning I checked out early in the morning and headed for the hotline heard about so much. I missed this lotto. Having no place to stay I took a chance on the other lotto at the Hostility House. I made this one. This is where I discovered the awful rotten and smelly ultimate truth of being the kind of lost victim to homelessness in such a cold cruel environment. But there I lay and slept. More nights on this floor and every morning going to hotline with high hope of making the lotto there paid off just in time for the coming of another GA check. This began the getting of hotline hotel rooms to keep from paying any rent when GA checks came. I could spend more on crack and in fact spent all checks ever achieved on crack. This pattern of living continued for a couple of months. Information is passed on through listening to others and inquiring. Through both methods I found the Tenderloin self-help center where I soon became a volunteer. Another TL help office, north of The Coalition, operated a small newspaper called the Homeless Mink. I wrote articles about being homeless and addicted and my feelings about it all. The editor and I became very good friends and in fact she had fallen in love. I knew being a sexual 'deviant' and addicted that I was on my way to prison. I would have frustrated this wonderful lady to no end. I felt love for her as well. At the self-help center I wrote other articles for their newsletter and became involved with the program of help for the homeless. My involvement soon got me a paid position with this organization. Another job and another paycheck, larger than that of GA, were again my worst enemy and my addiction's best friend. Two paychecks later and I was again at the GA office reapplying. Hotline hotels continued through it all for reasons already known. There were a number of reapplications for GA.

Each time was also the acquiring of GA hotels allowing me a break from hotline. But because my addiction was now long out of control working for a living only meant working for the maintenance of an addiction to crack and nothing else. I had been initiated at VG, a housing project area not far from the Fallen hotel. I remember purchasing many times there. All those I met and smoked with were only passing occasions at VG. There were trips to the VG from the hotel on Polk Street during my hay-day on another of many short runs or episodes using crack. Hey; don't ask me why I went on what were the many episodes or better yet runs? Had to be the need for a two or three day or week or whatever cooling off period before getting right back on such a hard road. RC took me to VG during the several times I mentioned smoking with him and his buddies after release from jail. Doesn't matter what someone does to you: robs you, steals from you, gaffels you (sells you fake dope), burglarizes your home, steals from your mother, father, sister, brotha, kids, wife, steals your wife, husband or virtually any and everything. As long as he or she has an apology in the form of some crack all is forgiven. Believe me I am totally serious about this. You yourself will steal, rob, betray or whatever else from your family and closest relationships to get just one more damn hit! So RC, even though I could easily despise him, was forgiven for all his trickery and disrespect to me by smoking a tiny twenty dollar rock, better known as kibble, as a token of his false sorrow for my having gotten busted for snatching that purse and his occupying my abode while I was in jail. Guess this makes me one of those toss-ups who will do virtually anything for just one more hit as I thought I was completely done with RC. Our involvement dissolved quickly after the move from Polk. But the return trips to VG continued for the purchase of rocks. There are storage rooms in these project area units turned into smoke rooms. After purchasing some crack it is very convenient to use these rooms to sooth the eager, anxious, nervous craving for a hit. Out of a dozen of these dens not one is empty on an average day of crack dealing in this project—a project only one square block in size. Drive by shootings had been the talk of this hood just before my arrival in the city. This created a very popular name for the VG among the gangsters and gallant crack addicts which caused me to steer clear of it for a few months into the city. When GA and hotline hotels allowed me the whole check I remember purchasing crack at VG on several occasions by myself after having been escorted and introduced to the better deals found buying crack. The Fallen hotel I remember was a hotline hotel. As mentioned hotline hotels must be endorsed by the occupant by five o'clock that evening or lost to someone on a waiting list. It was GA day and I had been to VG that afternoon purchasing a hundred dollars' worth of crack. In route to the Fallen hotel to claim my room I met a youngster who had been hunting me with his eyes hoping I would say anything. A smile and a simple hello cued him to strike up a conversation and found us in my hotel room just that fast. Such a passing fancy did not even keep name exchange in memory. Crack did the usual and exhausted the supply in the usual short period of time. One thing I did that rarely occurs was my retaining over fifty dollars cash from the GA check. It was on! I met a couple in the building of the Fallen hotel who helped out with the cleaning of the hotel. They were smokers as well. Jan and Tom lived in a room in the rear of the hotel giving them better comfort to smoke in. I approached Tom about his knowledge of where to find a rock at two in the morning. An affirmative reply began another 'friendship', this time with these janitors of the Fallen hotel, after his return from VG with about thirty dollars' worth of crack from the fifty dollar bill I gave him. Purchasing crack at this time of night can never assure the kind of quantity or quality compared to day time hours. In fact night time is the right time for robbers, gaffelers and thieves in general. There were several occasions I experienced a hotline stay at the Fallen smoking with Tom and his toss-up Jan.

Just a block down the street from the Fallen hotel on Market was the Livic Center Hotel achieved again through hotline. The procedure to this destination was the same having stopped at the VG to cop and check in by the five o'clock deadline. Instead of meeting someone to smoke with at the VG I met a fella by the name of Fred in the TL. Smoking crack alone for me is an impossibility. This is because of the paranoia that sets in due to the rush experienced after ingesting the first hit. After that rush of the first hit there is virtually the demand for such a blast just that fast as such does not last long at all—a few minutes at the most. The deep fear of a heart attack threatens me to the point of total paranoia and fear. All I need to do to rid myself of this paranoia is to find someone, preferably a male sex partner to smoke with. I found Fred at a porno shop on the corner of sixth and mission just across the street from the Shelta hotel. An older man in his mid-forties, well maintained, very dark, tall and of course well-endowed caused my inviting him into a booth to watch a porno show and smoke a hit of crack. It was one of the more enjoyable times on crack which makes the addiction even stronger as one will search endlessly to find such rarity so sex related to the crack high. Many negative incidents occur during such an endless journey. I never stayed at the Livic Center again. Guess I wanted to keep this memory rather sacred. This is one of the greatest, probably the main reason why addiction to drugs, especially crack, gets so intense. Sex is foremost on the user's mind but the sex is more times detoured or spoiled by the craving for that ultimate blast—a blast achieved only during the first round. All other crack during any such smoking sessions tend to be linked to that first hit which gets in the way of the sex drive felt so heavily with the first and uttermost hit. Times like the Livic Center encounter are rarities. Paranoia and its counterparts search endlessly for again that ultimate blast and the way sex integrates with such intense volume. One other very pleasant experience in a hotline hotel located somewhere on and Turk was the Jarfile. Again I made the five o'clock deadline and smoked all but about seventy five dollars and a couple of twenty dollar rocks. It was late in the evening around eleven PM. I had two twenty rocks left because of the paranoia of smoking alone. After several times walking the halls, making fictitious bathroom runs and walking the immediate hall area outside my room I finally ran into a fella name Ernie. It was easy to see as well as feel the vibes for the same desire—company and a hit of sex related crack. I gladly offered to smoke a rock with him. He gladly accepted and invited me to his room located to my surprise next door to me. He even smoked his last hit with me. He talked for a few minutes and I ask if he could cop a couple more rocks in the area. Such was accomplished there in the hotel of good quality and quantity. Sex was the result and it was a very enjoyable tweek free night. Morning had opened our eyes to another day. Ernie is an older man about 45 years old of particular bi-sexual character which excited my fancy and passion for those conservative folks like me. His dislike and disgust for flaming faggots did not match that of mine as I will indeed make friends with my gay family of this nature but sex does not arouse me. We could have become very close friends and even lovers but I never saw him again. My taste for a sex partner has always been an older man. One more hotline room was achieved at the Jarfile but no crack or sexual encounters were sought. I was in a heavy stage of wanting very much to get my life away from crack and had been on a dry run for another of those few days during times staying at the Jarfile. I also attribute successful and enjoyable relationships or encounters such as Ernie a help factor in coming to such thinking about my life on crack. But such a pattern of thinking was short lived. Such a memory made the craving and urges for another run on crack in search for someone like Ernie or Ernie himself pretty hard to deal with. The Cassador hotel around the corner from the Jarfile located on the corner of Mason and Eddy streets continued the tweeking on crack. At this hotel I remember more than just one stay. There was hotline, GA and my living standards for that short time. Seems during the transition to the final destination on Polk Street there was a sort of lay over for a night while in search for the place at the Polk Street residence. This lay-over was the first of three experiences at the Cassador hotel—another of the many nasty hotels in the TL. I expressed my desire to move from the Plotter hotel on ninth and Mission to my boss when I held the receptionist position. Barbara advanced me a couple hundred dollars which was a personal loan from her back then. I owed a few weeks rent at the Plotter and they wanted me out but not as bad as I wanted out. With the money loaned to me I left for the Bladiator hotel. Payday was a day away and I moved to the Cassador until such time. This was an even deeper hotter spicier taste of the Tenderloin. It was less than a two day stay at the Cassador. Here I met a toss-up who copped for me. We had worked together selling those light bulbs. I also met a brotha name WB who accompanied me on one of many tweeking journeys. Some fifty or sixty dollars and two runs for more dope by the toss-up who lived in the Cassador all began the tweeking turned into straight up geeking. WB had become so paranoid until his rapport spoiled and infected both me and Helen—the toss-up. There was still a good supply of crack on the plate when Helen had gone to cop more dope. It was so weird how WB tweeked out to the point beyond the peephole on the door and constant searching for crumbs and pebbles even though enough dope was available. His finale came when he picked up the plate of crack and casually walked to the closet door and tossed the rocks on the plate in the closet after which he shut the closet door. Looking around the room with an even crazier empty expression on his face he brought the plate back, sat it down and just looked into space. That had to be the ultimate show of paranoia ever witnessed. Seems he may have been fighting to say "no"! Well the crack was salvaged but his actions continued to be the tweek of the century. It was time to rid myself of dude. A twenty dollar bill and instructions to go cop ended the tweek of WB as he couldn't get back in the hotel without paying a five dollar after-curfew-guest fee. Meanwhile Helen had made it back and we laughed into tears about WB's tweekin' condition, after which she give me oral sex. The next day was the move to Polk Street. The second experience at the Cassador was one that include crack but it was only a taste provided by Helen. This was one of the times I achieved a hotline hotel for shelter's sake only. It was not a GA payday and I had no money. Helen knew I was the kind to come up more than being a downer freak. She knew of the jobs held as a telemarketer and the receptionist position. And now I had reapplied for GA and the Cassador was a GA hotel spot. She knew I would get a check during a time of month no one else had funds—not that of GA which was the general norm. So she smoked a twenty with me and like the prior encounter after my getting rid of WB I accepted oral sex from her. But when the act of total sex had come too close I could not perform. The final encounter at the Cassador was a notable one for me. I was awakened to a roach that seem to be quite the nightmare theatre size crawling on my chest. I knew this place was filthier than I had known filth to be. Waking to a roach crawling on me scared the living hell out of me. My classy northwestern ghetto rearing saw very few roaches. In fact I really never knew what a roach actually looked like except that they are brown in color and resembled a bigger version of an ant. There was only one house I remember as a child we moved into that had roaches. Mom moved out within a matter of days before our furniture and such became infested with these creatures. I had never in my life seen a roach more than an inch in size until San Francisco's Cassador hotel where I woke to one at least this size crawling on me. Getting oriented into a life of such degradation with its filth; roaches, rats, drugs, mental neglected illness, disease and all other counterparts of such a life in the Tenderloin was indeed becoming the reality I never realized at that time. Jumping up from the single bed in this hotel room that came equipped without sheets, but with a worn blanket, a broken window, hallway toilets and showers of the smallest nastiest condition; I began slapping my chest which was instant reaction from being frightened of a monster I just knew was my doom. Helen came over and smoked a twenty with me. She calmed and soothed me by explaining how roaches of size were common and not to be frightened of them. Roaches were part of the ghetto life in places like the Tenderloin. Her words relieved me a great deal but I could not perform for her as we had done in the past. Nor could I or will I ever be totally unafraid of roaches of such size. That was the last time I had sex with Helen, even though I smoked with her a couple times after. As time continued on in the TL I became more at ease at the site of roaches. And I saw many thousands of them—even those of enormous size. I never woke to another roach crawling on my body again—thank goodness. But they take showers with you, eat your food, and crawl on your plate of dope—hey! I ain't supportin' yo' habit—, hang around your counter tops, bathrooms (if you have one) on your toilet, sink and toothbrush, your clothes and virtually everything. There have been many times I had to knock roaches off my pants or jacket after putting them on as they were there before getting dressed. Becoming use to roaches was quick and somewhat easy aided by the need for shelter and a place to advance my addiction. The experiences and episodes in the Tenderloin culturing the gut of addiction occurred with the first experience at the Cassador in August 1988 just before the three month run on Polk Street. After the three month run came the continued living in the TL for some months before finally getting sentenced to prison. The roaches experienced at the Cassador did not frighten me away because I achieved a hotline room which continued on through GA. In other words when the GA contract of seven days was up I had made the lotto at hotline which just so happen to be the Cassador. So all I did was move from one hotel room into another in the same hotel. Add to this a GA check on that seventh day. After cashing the check and sending Helen to purchase some crack I found myself again in the site of a good looking stranger who lived in the building. Why in the hell do they always come along when your pockets are fat? Can they smell and sense like a dog? Frank was about five feet ten, approximately 170 pounds, very dark complexion and solid as a rock. I had moved one floor down right next door to him. Having rid myself of my pacifier, Helen, with a twenty and a promise I was now free to take that walk on the wild gay side. This ended about three AM that morning. All dope was consumed. The infection of paranoia had infiltrated the both of us and his disappearance left no memory of ever having even the thought of sex which was again and again the usual consequences. Seems that rare times with a successful encounter are paid for as the search for another such memory becomes a battle lost more times than not. Many more of these very same consequences with faces having no names helped to consume the many twenty dollar rocks in the TL. Those remembered are of special quality and feelings that made up the file in my memory coming out into focus in this kind of evaluation of a particular and very intense part of my life. Another episode occurred at the Scalding hotel where the star salesman, PV, of the telemarketing outfit lived. He had invited me over to his place one Saturday afternoon after work. Guess my name had gotten around. Saturdays at this job are paydays. Consequently we both had money. I mentioned my desire for an older man in the 35-45 year old bracket. PV introduced me to an older man who was six feet plus inches tall, approximately 175 pounds, a gray close cut full beard and mustache with close cut hair to match, very well dressed and oh yah 55 years old. Top it all off with his having been spoiled rotten because of his fancy good looks all his life. Even worse is his having been a crack addict many more years than I believe I could actively be. That statement is the very reason these writings come before me in print as part of what is termed my personal inventory. So let it out if you can follow enough of your thoughts on paper—let it all out! Slim and I became road dogs for a bit. Only I was the stupid puppy trying to get next to him sexually. My money sure felt the pain of wanting this old cunning good looking rock star. Our encounters smoking and my continued paranoia tweeking with Slim carried on from time to time beginning at the Scalding to the Shelta and Sauburn hotels located within very short walking distance from each other in the TL. Guess PV paid me back for EJ. I know he wanted EJ but 'Potna' was very paranoid of PV's thin size and his wearing a wig? Paranoia and fear of PV being HIV positive plagued EJ. Slim lasted a long time. I smoked with him as mentioned every so often over this time lasting some six or eight months. But his knowledge of my wanting him and my intense desire turning into paranoia for him caused us to tweek whenever we encountered each other. More adventures, episodes and their experiences continued in the hotline and occasional GA acquired hotels all in the TL and outlining areas where both hotline and GA have contracts with more of the community for this kind of poverty stricken existence. The hotel located on Eddy Street between Jones and Leavenworth was an interesting experience. Even though I lived there through the system on occasion; this was not that occasion. It involved a gay brotha, Marti, who was into his early stage of addiction as I was but further along than myself. We had met at the self-help center in the TL on Golden Gate Street. It was during the time I had got a paid position after volunteering. Marti also acquired a paid spot and for the month of this job's existence we hung together as road dogs. Only crack was our drug of choice not heroin as the case usually may be with the formation of 'road dogs' during this era (1980s). Road dogs can stay more on top of feeling the high a lot longer while a crack monster smokes up everything searching for that ultimate beginning high thus always falling flat. There was a time Marti invited me to his hotel along with several other fellas for a smoke out, compliments of him. He bought some crack and began a series of paranoid and tweeking events. The reason this was so noticeable for me is because of the pattern of his tweeking. Marti became oddly involved and obsessed with hiding rocks that were not there. In other words he never hid these imaginary rocks he continually searched for on window ledges, ledges over the door, all apart of those beams and ledges of the hotel room. He also looked under the rugs, mattress, chairs and other seemingly good hiding places to stash that "last hit". In the past I had seen and been infected by searching like this for crumbs, dust and such in the carpet and other similar places. Marti became totally engulfed by this making me shy away from his paranoia instead of becoming infected by it. It was not contagious with him. His behavior pattern seemed to be caused by the company he had invited who would not pursue his sexual desires, which help lead him into this kind of behavior. I myself have been paranoid by the intense desire for someone, Slim, and could not get the act of sex initiated causing the 'how do I get the sex object sexually aroused?' syndrome to spoil an evening and hundreds of dollars in crack. He too would continue to make those runs and go on late night missions for more crack in order to retain the company of what was still hoped to be a sexual encounter wanted so bad. I left during Marti's time of sexual crisis. Other times smoking crack with Marti and others, of his luring, saw the exact same pattern now a routine. This is another example of an addiction to crack on a very speedy rise. I rarely mentioned Oakland during all the ten months in the Tenderloin.

Oakland was a place heard about way back home and my curiosity took me there several times purchasing crack. EJ, his brotha VC and I drove there one sunny Saturday afternoon while on one of the three-month runs I experienced. We bought some crack of again size and quality which lasted long into the night. EJ has four brothas of which I met two. It was easy to see the effects of crack infiltrating our black society in especially the ghetto. A couple more trips to Oakland acquired me knowledge of where to cop which came later after prison that were also disappointing experiences. One disappointing saga was the years of my work in art brought with me to San Francisco from Seattle. At one of many nights spent in Frisco after running out of money it hit me how I just may be able to sell my work. Desperate for another blast of dope I gathered all fourteen canvas works and made it back to the dope house I found so quickly earlier this same night. Well; to tell you what I remember only comes with the one or two hits for each canvas. Being able to wait for paydays, be they payroll or GA, had been challenged by Satan and quickly becoming his victory. The position at telemarketing is where I met a fella name Joe who introduced me to a dealer name Mike. Can't remember where I met Joe but I do know it was around, not in, the Hostility House during the time of being a telemarketer. I was not introduced into the Hostility House. I only knew of it through the usual gossip. I believe Reggie may have had a hand in Joe and I being introduced as Reggie and I did travel to the TL a number of times to cop when business was bad in the Fillmore. Joe introduced me to Mike who worked the Golden Marches on seventh and Market as it was a popular cop spot. Mike and I did a lot of business together even to the point of traveling to HP, again the biggest crack alley in the city. Joe reaped the rewards for such a good connection. He smoked a lot of crack with me. We even went to Oakland on an occasion. He worked in a gay bar they called Sable's cliff located somewhere on Telegraph. This was another experience I must explore. My lust for company, sex and all the negative friends kept me in these kinds of situations with basically the same consequences—of course. This one began in San Francisco as I listened to Joe paint a picture of this black gay bar in Oakland with an exciting paint brush that got my undivided attention. It was still winter although spring was just around the corner. With about 150 bucks to spend I was pitched by Joe about the size and quality of 35 dollar rocks. Size and quality for early progressing crack addicts is a sure sales application and as well keeps the mark unaware or just plain stuck on stupid. The crack he purchased in Oakland for the 35 dollar price was not any bigger in size and quality than the twenty dollar rocks found in the TL. In fact a better deal could have been achieved in the VG or even better HP. But the excitement of the city in Oakland and the fun soon to happen at the black gay bar kept my being eaten alive and burned by Joe a misdemeanor. Crack cocaine contains a host of chemicals said to cause the paranoia and other effects from is use. I can believe this because I never felt any of these effects when I shot the powder form of cocaine back home. Smoking away all the money including years of art work in Oakland with Joe and finally going to the bar found me completely tweeked out. I could do nothing but sit in one spot for hours in this paranoid state and listen to the mad rhythm that made me so popular in the gay bars on the dance floor back home. Such was not the case at this black gay bar thus I got up enough whatever to ask Joe to advance me the few bucks needed for a bus back to San Francisco. Directions were also needed by him to find this bus. The Bart subway station was closed but an all-night bus was available running in very long intervals. I waited for about two hours in the bay area night from about one to three AM. Finally getting back to San Francisco was a relief and found me very soon in bed and fast asleep. This experience in Oakland with Joe was not the pleasant affair I had been convinced it would be. I do recall the magical wonderful rhythm of the many favorite funky groups who got my undivided attention back home on especially the dance floor now heard in such a paranoid state of being in addiction. Another incident with Joe was the introduction of the Solumbia hotel in the TL around O'Farrell Street. I met a toss-up name Kitty who had been a resident of this crack hotel for a number of years. Here again I spent all money smoking with Joe and this toss-up. But this was the final experience and end of a so called 'potnaship' although our paths crossed many times in the TL. You might say he continued to try his luck to lure me into another hopeless affair with him. All I could see in his face was the sorrow I felt and the pitiful condition I was in at Sable's Cliff in Oakland. The many months of an adventure in the TL saw a number of trips with its expenses to Oakland copping crack. A Bart subway ride to the west Oakland stop found a site just around the corner where I copped a few times. Another time I went to Oakland with a fella from the Solumbia in San Francisco whose name I don't remember. He too drew this huge picture of quality and size for the hundred bucks I spent with his connection that beautiful spring day in 1989. Instead of introducing me to his connection he told me to wait outside because his connection did not take kindly to anyone new. This was told to me after the trip to Oakland. But; like the dump, zip-damn fool I was I gave him the hundred bucks and it took him some time to cop. I thought he had ran off and I again was burnt—another form of gaffled. But after about 45 minutes he showed up with yet another gaffel situation. I know now what he had done. He copped the crack, left dude's apartment, chipped pieces from the five rocks, probably what was in fact worth fifty dollars—all five hits now of ten dollar size. If someone is bold enough to burn you like this and return with the ole "how do you like these bolders?" line the best thing to do is escape his company as soon as possible. Such a bold move by him could have very well led to robbery, a fight, stabbing or even worse—murder. Who knows if dude had a gun, knife or any weapon of some kind? We made Bart back to San Francisco and the Solumbia hotel where I made up an excuse of retrieving a toss-up and would be right back. It was months before I saw him again—good ridden! Speaking of turning a situation with drugs into violence reminds me of a hotel in Frisco called the City Spinter somewhere on Hyde Street. I had eighteen bucks and wanted a hit.

This is another time I left my better judgment in reserve, if I even had such a tool at this point, with another fella whose name was not known due to not even exchanging any words of a normal introduction. He knew where I could get a fat twenty for the eighteen dollars. Little did I know he too was tweeking and in just as much, if not more, need of a hit then I. Because it was day, not night, I went with him to the City Spinter, another ghetto hotel in the TL which at that time was in the local and public news for its many one room units being rented to families of four or more. There had been no major catastrophe such as an earthquake to warrant this kind of intense hotel living. Many of these tenants had vacated and others yet to leave leading to this hotel's final closure. This dude took me to the sixth floor of this shack. The hotel seemed like a ghost town already with the many empty rooms—more empty than occupied. He took me into an abandon room and proceeded to ask for the money so he could go cop. Not my last eighteen bucks! I just wasn't going for it. I told dude to get potna and bring him to the room. After being gaffeled so much in the past I was not going to let my last hit go just like that. Luck was with me because he thought he could bully the money out of me without having to fight. This meant he had no weapon. Add to this his being much thinner than me. I have never been thin. My average 200 pounds at 5'10" made him pretty leery of trying to really test my coward bell. But he indeed tried the raised voice move. He yelled at me in a mean tone for me to give him the money or I would "get my ass kicked". "No way dude"; I replied. He could see that I was somewhat frightened from the beginning going up to the room with him having noticed the haunted-house atmosphere. But to hell with the Adams Family shack effects he tried to create. Dude was not getting my last few dollars. He swung at me and the punk missed. He then grabbed a piece of a clothes hanger from the floor. It was stem wire which was about six inches long having been turned into a pusher that accommodates a scud missile used to clean and push the screen that melts the rock. The dude was more scared now than I had been and began showing it after I would not show fear of his demands and grabbing such a meek weapon. I charged him and we scrapped very loosely on the box spring mattress on the floor. This had turned into a funny scene because dude had no win over me. I kicked him a couple of times and simply pushed him away from me. When he saw that my money was not obtainable and that a few more minutes could very well find him a victim of rape or something just as strange due to the thoughts haunting my Dr. Jeckel/Mr. Hyde personality caused by the atmosphere he brought me to, he backed off me and offered his truce. But I personally did not want a truce. I had begun exploring his body and in doing so I became sexually excited having created an erection. Now; if I were one of many deviants of rape there would have been no mention of truce or even the silly little battle we encountered in this perfect set-up for such a crime. Poor dude; he must have felt like a complete idiot as well as his being scared to death. He should have known that the city he was addicted in was full of freaks. He was young, good looking and weaker than me. This incident ended in his shaking my hand in what was indeed a truce anyway and apologizing. I would have gladly smoked the eighteen bucks with him as he needed a hit but dude flew the coop in one great big flash leaving me there with my deviant thoughts of him. Guess he learned a lesson—I didn't. Wonder if such an experience scared him straight? Hope it did anyway as I look back on this one experience. That bit of violence mixed with comedy was not a lesson for me as it only intensified my lust for a hit and now some sex. Don't know the outcome of that day but you can bet I wound up in bed alone and even worse sexually frustrated with only eighteen dollars thought to satisfy both cravings. I may have even gotten gaffeled still yet. I found through experience that getting gaffeled more often happens when one is down to the very last twenty, ten and sometimes fifty dollars. The reason for this is because the end of funds creates a very anxious search for that last hit. To spend the last fifty dollars means to get the best deal possible even though this final mission is the one that always occurs at the peak hours and beyond that of 'late night' where gaffelers have a hayday selling candle wax, vitamin b-12, ivory soap and the like along with straight up taking your money the second a weakness is revealed—similar to the turn around with dude in the haunted house. The final twenty, the search for a ten or the "yeah; I'll sell you a five shot" more times than not ends up in despair. There are many more experiences that make up the many months of addiction to crack based in the Tenderloin (TL). The experiences to this point give a general pattern of how my addiction to such a new-wave drug in such as the ghetto of the Tenderloin in San Francisco, California tore my life apart. It gave me no chance to stop and try growing into someone positive—although thoughts and mere tries were prompted. Seems I had to go through this crazy dilemma. The traps I fell so willingly into led me through the hell that could still be just as horrible a nightmare today as were the many yesterday's hopelessly lost and ignorant to a way out of drugs and into a positive new feeling for life. I started a series of tries and attempts at sobriety. All were not done straight from the heart. If they were from the heart such attempts were lost with much of the velocity of the 100 percent needed to make that real move toward the victory of actually saying no. My addiction fought to win the many victories there were at making the many attempts to stop. But again these honest attempts were not the needed power to fight something I thought would only be temporary abstaining and doing it better the next time—a syndrome suffered during much of the addiction to its end. Such a thought pattern was used only to get myself out of the problems suffered for only whatever moment that had become too big for me to handle with simply quitting and getting out of the addiction. What is addiction anyway??? There were times crack had my heart so busted up with remorse and pity for myself that tries were taken more seriously—the Great Tide church. Dealing with them kept a strong beat and a growing desire to still become a success at life lasting only until the next defeat to the urges and cravings of crack cocaine. Thus the battle with crack continued which involved a war full of ammunition on both sides at the end of the time spent lost in the Tenderloin full of crack cocaine.

THE EFFECTS OF THE BLAST

EVA' THOUGHT ABOUT WHY ONE
GOOD BLAST DON'T LAST?

WELL, SUCKA', COULD BE THE PSYCHOLOGY
MASTERING YA IMMEDIATE PAST.

YA SEE; AFTA ONE GOOD HIT; YA THROW DOWN WIT';
AAHH SHHIITT, GOTTA GET ANOTHER LITTLE BIT!

NOW; THIS GOES ON UNTIL THE VERY END
WHEN THE INSANITY SAYS "HEY FOOL;
NOW!!! DO IT ALL OVER AGAIN!"

NOW CAN YA MAYBE SEE THE PSYCHOLOGICAL
PATTERN OF THE BLAST
AND WHY IT DON'T GIVE A SUCKA
THE SATISFACTION TO LAST?

IV

TeeLancey Exit Recovery Program

Fighting the decision to quit the use of crack saw many attempts that were victorious for the opposite side. I remember writing that began at the coalition center for the homeless link ghetto newspaper. It covered feelings of remorse, its counterparts of rejection and needed implementation for an emergency help center at Great Tide church as well as the crack rap written against its use. There are experiences that led to some of the better win situations during my stubborn road to free the prisoner in my addicted mind, body and soul. As mentioned high hope at Great Tide failed probably due to my not being completely willing to surrender. The high had become the habit and I was seeking a pacifier that could get attention enough or get it dealt with enough in context to deter thoughts of using. To have to hit my bottom again and again before I completely surrendered was not only Great Tide's philosophy but others who could help but were reluctant because of commitment. But there were many times I wanted out and wanted out for good.

I remember somewhat an experience that ended in an unusual way. I can't recall the hotel or if it was GA or hotline. What I recall was my decision to go to jail where I would be safe and able to clean my act up so I could begin an almost sure journey to recovery. I knew crack had left me completely 'shot to the curb' for another of so many times. I remember somewhat this night starting out with Tytan Street's jail turning myself in—or trying to. I had the feeling they could easily arrest me or get me to a drug detox program. But the opposite found threats by police in this jail saying they would arrest me for a more serious crime if I did not get the hell out of their site. I left but walked around the area and began something else along with purse snatching I thought never existed in me. I began setting fi res to dumpsters. After several fi res to dumpsters I left this area. But the night was far from finished. I was angry at the response of so-called law officers. Of course my wanting to be locked up was quite out the ordinary. But after telling my problem of drugs their rejection made me rather upset with vengeful thoughts. Seems they could have at least given direction to detox or shelters someplace or maybe even had a list available of help agencies to issue someone like me or those coming out of jail insistent upon giving up a life drugs, homelessness, crime and the like. I found myself in the Fillmore district tweeked out on crack in the cold rainy night near a police station on Webster Street. After entering their police station and telling an officer at the desk I was loaded on crack and if they had help programs available to seriously deal with crack addiction they too responded with rejection saying how I had gotten myself into such a trap and they were not baby sitters and could do nothing. Add to this the officer at the desk telling me to leave. I remember having been to the hospital some days earlier due to a seizure having caused me to hurt my leg. I was put on a cane. After leaving the Fillmore station in an even worse mental and emotional state of mind I walked outside this station's building. I noticed the lighting on the station's building. The revenge that entered my mind also solved the problem of walking around the area in a state of helplessness full of crack cocaine. With the cane I busted several of these lights on the wall of the Fillmore police station. This ended a tweeking night of misery and a place to get out of the cold night and maybe get my head back on my shoulders. Maybe in jail I could put a positive plan together—this time for sure. But this was only one of four arrests during my addiction in San Francisco. Deliberate cause to be taken off the streets included the vandalism at the Fillmore police station and the final arrest taking me to prison for a year were the major arrests I recall. Before getting to that arrest there is the third incident leading to some weeks spent in jail at the San Bruno site. This arrest was a true show of the stupidity and its effects that continue the cycle of crack cocaine. While on GA I was also getting food stamps. Money of all spendable source and kind is spent on crack. Food stamps can easily be sold for two thirds its value. On this particular day my date had arrived to pick up food stamps at the check cashing facility where GA checks are also claimed and cashed. After getting the food stamps I was looking for a cash buyer who would buy the 99 dollars' worth of stamps for the usual 65 dollars cash. Walking from the check cashing facility on O'Farrell I ran into a white man about 45 years old in blue jeans looking like a John searching for a prostitute as he was standing in front of a laundry mat in the area where prostitutes work. I was also with RC, of all people, who again pointed this dude out. I casually asked this man if he wanted to buy some food stamps and his reply was affirmative. But instead of pulling out any money to exchange hands he reached in the front neck of his shirt and pulled out a police badge attached to a chain. I was put under arrest and sent to San Bruno after conviction to do a six week sentence. Thus far crack had taken all sense of morals, love and self-esteem, pride, desire for life and positive growth and as well my entire positive self-worth turning it all into one big lusting passion for the very next GA payday, food stamps or any amount substantial enough to experience the false pleasure of that ultimate blast! During the stages where I began experiencing trouble with the law also began the growth of the 'want and desire to quit' factors a part of an arsenal still alive after so many defeats with the opposing side—my addiction. I remember detoxing at a place on Howard Street only to be let out the day GA checks came out. I only remember cashing that one particular check that day. Volunteer work at the self-help center began my working positively on self-esteem and began more and more thinking about the problems I faced being an addict during this period of peak homelessness. Their giving me a paid position ended all the work toward possible surrender and achievement of that higher entity needed in this war. There were shelters for a night here another there all due to having exhausted any and all funds including the loss of anymore chances at a job resorting to GA and food stamps which only wound up in a scud missile. A couple of months near the end of a year run in the Tenderloin began even greater and more intense feelings of remorse, pity, sorrow, rejection and an awesome continuous feeling of worthlessness. The vandalism at the Fillmore police station was one of the in-depth feelings that fought my addiction so intensely. Other times after smoking up more GA checks continued this war waged so deeply against crack. Here is where one of the many battles fought so hard saw great victory for the want and desire army—a battle the addiction lost!! I remember the date very well as it was on a GA payday—July 15th, 1989. It was night around seven o'clock and I had again been on a run having smoked up another GA check and still homeless. During this period near the very end of the ten to twelve month TL dilemma I would not achieve a hotline room. Why; I don't know. I just could not make it to the early AM hotline anymore. I slept in shelter after shelter, night after night all over the TL and other places I could find—some nights including the streets. The disease of homelessness had begun to seriously plague me. On this night of the 15th from a phone booth on 8th and Market at the Livic Center by the foundation I called the detox program at a hospital I frequented to try and gain admittance—something my army against the addiction in me did. This detox program was full and its waiting list was and probably still is more than three months long. I had tried Anaram before this call but the lady I talked to expressed this facility being a full to capacity situation. The more we talked the more desperate I became as I pleaded to this lady for some help now! It hit her that TeeLancey Exit Recovery Program may accept me in my condition. "Try it" is all she could advise. "Well; if I catch the five Fulton bus that you say will let me off at this place; will you do a great favor and please, mam, please call them for me and let them know I will be out there as soon as possible? Please mam" I begged and pleaded with tears flying from my eyes. She agreed to do so. The want and desire had done part of a first step by my admitting the need for help. I admitted being powerless and I knew my life was so unmanageable until it was a must to win this battle on this night. And win I did for it was only a few minutes after hanging up the phone to this lady that I was on the five Fulton bus to TeeLancey drug program. Some twenty minutes later I was sitting and waiting on an intake bench for some hours (what I want to call a kind of detox) before being taken in and interviewed by a small committee and bedded down on their from room floor. I guess there was no room in the dorms. That did not bother me at all. It was very comfortable and soothing and as well a relief to me. I just knew I had made the right move to fight and give up addiction to recovery. Little did I know this process of change does not just happen overnight with the help of a treatment facility. Upon entering the doors of TeeLancey Exit Recovery Program there were many people, about one hundred or so, dinning and preparing for their evening activities. The old style furniture matched the old style well-kept building. Small dining tables were set with table ware and cloth. Chairs matched the tables and there was a great big bar without stools directly in the front lobby area. It was not a wet bar stocked with liquor but a huge old style bar with long, thin circumference, dark wood cut trees used for foot rests mounted around the edge of the bar. A TV room with a 48 inch color screen set, a library downstairs, dorms upstairs, co-ed as well and cleanliness throughout made up this pleasant environment to recover in. But this was the atmosphere created by everything but the people in it. Upon entering TeeLancey Exit Recovery Program after asking for intake services I was told to sit on an intake bench where I sat for a number of hours waiting to be interviewed. My condition probably prompted this long wait. At the interview I found that sympathy and compassion were not innocent natural feelings to have in offering help for someone to find a life in recovery after a hard past using drugs. The usual questions of history, drug of choice, why I wanted sobriety, how I felt they could help, family and the like brought the story of my life into focus to them and my need and desire as well as want to become drug free. I was told in a tone that may have scared those not serious about such a facility how their program was part of a work therapy. They also put it to me that if I wanted sobriety I would work for it and ask me how serious I was about it. Tears did not seem to faze them. I was not crying to cop their compassion. There seem to be none. Satan may very well have been trying his hand in seeking a vain he could sink his fangs into. Expressing the failure found trying to do it on my own, my not completely surrendering, falling shy to excuse-seeking and how frustrated and frightened I had become brought those tears about. The entire interview frightened me. The thought of not being accepted and back out in the streets was a nightmare I hoped would not happen scaring me more than the interview itself. I thought about the people I saw during the waiting time on the intake bench and how happy there seemed to be. I noticed too how no one looked my way. It was my conclusion they had all been through the same thing and knew I needed this time to see clean and sober behavior and make up my mind to give it my best shot, which I did see and wanted very much—probably due to the awesome frightened condition I was in. I did see people having a wonderful time without drugs. I knew right then and there that work to gain a happy and successful status was a must. A sensation came over me of eager readiness for the hard work, mental, social and emotional change ahead. I remember both my two year associate degrees. They were no easy task. They were brought back to mind that night. I became more eager and more confident that I had made the best decision for my life at this point. I was going to make them proud of my success in the two year program outline of TeeLancey Exit Recovery Program where I would work and grow to become the clean and sober intelligent, good hearted person I wanted to be. It was a night of entertainment after the diner they had upon my arriving. A dance and stand-up comedy were highlights of the evening. The happiness witnessed saw eagerness to become successful in this program even more as I patiently waited for the interview and its results. After all the entertainment, outside people having departed and residents having retired for the night I was called to be interviewed. I was more or less reprimanded in what seemed a scolding tone about the program and desire for it. I was bedded in the front room due to, I guess, the problem of space at such an hour of the night. I noticed the chillier highlight of the interview which seem to cause their reluctance toward admitting my sexuality. But I opened up about this part of my life as well in expressing my life to them. The committee harped on this warning me of the program's strict policy on flaunting. Had I kept my sexuality out of my diseased addiction testimony, one of the main factors causing me to use, all may have went well with them and probably would have had a different effect or attitude toward me. This was seem by the sudden change in their attitude after my bringing up my sexuality and it being a major reason I kept relapsing and continuing to use crack cocaine and how I felt it being so related to the addiction. But for that night I was in and was told that a full committee would be held that next day deciding my acceptance or rejection into their program. Lying on the floor on a mat with sheets and warm blanket put me to sleep almost immediately. But for the few moments I was awake I felt very thankful for another chance and felt good about the unknown journey to sobriety in this strange new and very exciting land of positive opportunity. Having orally expressed my resume including not only prison but hard toil and just as hard a struggle to complete four years of college seemed to be a plus on my side. I could become motivated and generate new ground for myself in my quest for sobriety in such a positive environment. I thought of how my sexuality would be suppressed as it was a personal part of my life that would only be dealt with in hope of achieving a way out of the cycle of sex for drugs or rather relating so carelessly these two entities. Private counseling and therapy I had hopes of and felt confident about would be in the program outline of this program. Even though I was frightened after the interview that night I continued to feel love in the atmosphere of this new environment and felt good about ending a life trapped so blind and hopeless by the crack monster. The rough treatment I thought I was getting in the interview was thought to be their way of letting me know that the program was no easy task. Thinking ahead like this may have been positive or it may have been wishful thinking. Whatever the case may have been I wanted to make this program work. I knew I was very serious about the thoughts taken to sleep with me at the end of that day. The next day I began seeing life lived in the residence of TeeLancey Exit Recovery Program. I was awakened at approximately five in the morning to the preparation of breakfast. I forgot the name of the process used but every resident/client has days assigned where they serve the meals to the others of the program including staff. Instead of forming a long line there is a team of waiters who wait their assigned tables. This is an everyday process. The summer mornings at TeeLancey Exit Recovery Program were warm with bright and shinning sun sparkling on the building. The atmosphere was even warmer as a result. The continuing first day of this program found me in the conference room in front of a full committee that let me know of my having been accepted. More reprimand concerning my sexuality was again relayed. I was given two days a week to wait tables and given other job assignments. I only remember the last two nights of the twelve day experience at TeeLancey Exit Recovery Program sleeping in a dorm. I believe they were reluctant to put me in with other people, men, even though my own commitment to this program put any sexual play completely under lock and key. There was a room downstairs on the main floor I slept in with a couple others new to the program on my first night in this dorm. This they called phase steps before being advanced to a dorm upstairs. Everybody in this program before me had left for the permanent dorms. Others behind me also went to these dorms upstairs. I did not make an issue of this at all. I only noticed it and concluded the very possible reason why I was still in this room downstairs. After all I had been determined to make this work. Job assignments and the complete therapy made up approximately eighteen hours a day. From five AM to eleven PM is a regular day, every day except whatever day off was allowed. I believe it took a number of weeks to earn the one day off. I remember working in the front living room on the janitorial crew. TeeLancey Exit Recovery Program lasted exactly twelve days. Morals, beliefs, emotional pressure, prejudices, hatred and my own limited tolerance crushed all the determination to make this program in TeeLancey Exit Recovery Program work for me. There was no problem with the long hours at work from five to five. The hard work found me sweating—something I became aware of very quickly that was very good for me. I felt good about it having the theme of "gotta get this crack out of me" as part of my work therapy. Work quickly became the habit in place of crack. Was I actually substituting one for another? The people there are an interesting part of the program. Everyone there from staff of the highest degree to newcomers have been through or had yet to complete the program. Even the committee members that interviewed me are successful graduates of this program. Counselors, cooks and virtually all who operate the program are in recovery. Of course the bulk of the residents are those addicts like me. Many are ex-convicts as well. Doing two years as part of the program outline did not scare me at all. Paranoia began setting in along with fear as I became the victim of "Games"! Another term for Games is exactly what Games implies—attack therapy. This kind of war game therapy was not the kind of recovery I had in mind. In fact it is not something I could deal with. Attack therapy is a venting of frustration, anger and the like in a small group setting of approximately a dozen clients who vent their hate and anger out on each other. This type of therapy is supposed to be a way of breaking an individual down mentally and emotionally or whatever else in an effort to rebuild a brand new positive person. This method of therapy work may have worked if not for my sexuality known by the residents of the program. Can't say who put the word out of if someone there knew me and knew of my sexuality prior to TeeLancey Exit Recovery Program but the news of a "faggot" in the place infecting everyone with AIDS sure spread like a gasoline explosion. I felt their knowledge of this after a couple days into the program. I was rejected and avoided almost totally except for staff and work crew authorities assigning me jobs. My having epilepsy made matters even worse for me. On the third night I was scheduled to attend this new experience for me called Games. I had the idea that groups were formed for us to simply get together and rap about our lives and addiction, get to know each other and develop strength among us in our endeavors to find recovery. On this third night I had already been black balled being looked at with eyes of hatred toward my being that of a sexual deviant off ender. My name came up on the list on this third morning for the Games that night at seven sharp. I thought about how I could win these people over with all the positive ability I knew I possessed in an effort to deter my being looked at with such hatred for being gay. No Dice! At seven o'clock upon setting up and opening up this first Games session I was the center of attraction after about twenty minutes for those others who needed to relieve and vent their frustrations. I guess this was a way to let me know what I was in for since I had never been part of such attack therapy. Hatred for my being what I am was thrown in my face like pure dog shit smeared and rubbed in slowly and very piercing. I was called faggot after punk and degraded to the max. I was asked how I could live with myself being a faggot. I was accused of having AIDS which I did not have. In other words the entire group purposely misjudged me out of hatred for what I was and used this time to surprise and shock me into the truth about the main reason why one can be so frustrated at the end of the therapy called Games. This kind of treatment and the news of their true feelings toward me did not set well at all. I was very, very hurt and remained down in the dumps after biting my tongue to any rebuttal this first and second sessions of Games. At the second and continuing session there were more of the very same hatred coming my way. I was a victim of their dumping on me. This caused a progressive pattern of sorrow, self-pity, remorse, hatred for myself and a complete negative feeling of self, including a progressing paranoid feeling caused by the look on everyone's face of disgust and hatred toward me—all recent feelings I thought would be gone from my life as a result of this program. Arguments of several kinds among a couple fellas both Black and White were victorious for them. I was the center of the problem whatever it was, it didn't matter. Ridicule and its gossip continued the progressive pattern of paranoia. Every hour, minute and second became filled with fear.

Times in these increments became much longer. The end of the fourth day seemed two weeks long. The nurse seemed to be against me as well. Was I that much poison to all? If not for the "stop Nate; wait just a damn minute" part of me that had not become crushed by the ugly tone now the atmosphere in TeeLancey Exit Recovery Program, I may have had an even worse outcome. "I don't have to take this shit. I am human just like they are; and I'm not the only 'faggot' in the world". I have been told too many times that we all are subject to and in fact do make mistakes. So why was I the ideal victim of all this ridicule? Maybe I was the perfect scape goat. Maybe I was a mirror many of them looked in being a symbol of their own wrongs in which they could vent out hatred through me. But I had enough to worry about to carry their burdens. Games occur twice during the weekdays. I am not sure what went on during the weekend as I was there only two weekends frustrated by the program by the end of the twelve days. I had been plugged, given advice by someone in the program who I thought was sympathetic and compassionate telling me to vent my frustration right back at them. This compassionate person instead had plotted my eventual misfortune at TeeLancey. During the waiting time for meeting number three I began returning ugly looks of hatred while preparing to rebut their show of hatred which was not a step toward recovery—at least not for me. To change was something I knew had to happen along with recovery. To do it like this seemed so out of the norm. I even thought about how this could all be part of a change in my life desperately needed. To do it through the changing of my sexuality could not happen then and see no way of it happening now. Today as I write, I am still a gay man looking to someday in recovery encounter a relationship free of 'yesterday'. Until then I refrain from any encounter as was found during addiction. When the third meeting came I was a total emotional, nervous wreck. Working with others was like working alone except for being told what to do and the job not being right. I remember being assigned the laundry room. At the end of that day's very uncomfortable work environment with another resident I was hit with a list of things I supposedly had done wrong. Residents complained of clothes not being washed, others not folded and others not put in the right laundry sacks among other things supposedly done wrong that only conveyed my being a misfit and nothing I did was done right—a way added to get rid of me that became my thinking pattern. Another job assignment was in the basement stocking, shipping/receiving and general upkeep and cleaning of the basement's supply room and maintenance area. One argument came about with one resident who had been talking behind my back and teasing me about my sexuality. It appeared by his calling me "punks" and "homosexuals" that he wanted to fight me. The term 'punk' has always been a fighting word of slander in my book. I took every precaution including biting my tongue to prevent any disturbance but I could hold back no longer after his insistent calling me out to a duel. I rebutted with a few choice four letter words and a play of the 'dozens' which degraded his family as he had done to me. He began a loud rage of name calling and cussing in an attempt to draw immediate attention to those head figures of the facility. His aim was to make me look like the bad guy completely at fault without having to fight as he was noticeably lighter and a few inches shorter than I. This was another reason I tried to keep from fighting him. His plan worked as I was reprimanded for causing a potentially violent incident and how it was the quickest way to be expelled from the program. I was separated from this person and given a new job assignment scheduled for the next day. The day of this incident was the tenth day at TeeLancey Exit Recovery Program. Two more days remained before the end of what had turned into a nightmare. On this tenth day was also the day my name had come up on the list to attend group number three. I was also finally moved to the dorms upstairs much to everyone's disgust and my surprise. My being mentally frustrated, nervous and emotionally wrecked all creating an angry pattern of thought about a program I had so much confidence in found me eager to begin the rebuttal of their hatred for me through my own venting right back at them. I have never been in an in-house, inpatient recovery program. I had never sought help for an addiction because crack cocaine was the first insane, crazy, frightening and helpless addiction ever experienced to such a point all during my youth except for prison where I became serious minded and worked so hard in school. Having tried heroin I could have easily been a junky much earlier than now. I had to wait until almost forty years old to become addicted to a drug more popular than all other drugs of its time—another marijuana era multiple times more intense. No wonder I had made a success out of the ten years spent in prison. It was not difficult to put forth the effort to excel especially with the ways and means to do so at such easy access. Cigarettes were even easy to quit for the years I did during all the good fortune in education and art behind bars. Thus a need for something like TeeLancey Exit Recovery Program never crossed my mind back then. How was I to know what programs of this nature consisted of? How was I to know I would be living and dealing with people on an everyday basis who were just as sick as me? How I to know my sexuality was would be a critical focal point in dealing with recovery? Views from an un-orientated point saw a facility designed to "help any addict who wanted to quit; quit". During the nightmare with crack I did not really focus attention on quitting and when time began making me think more and more about quitting I had dug myself into what seemed a hopeless grave. Here in the environment of TeeLancey Exit Recovery Program for the twelve days I was there I learned so much about being honest, sincere, wanting success and working for it along with others striving for the same thing. Little did I know competition would wreck me in a place like this having no knowledge of handling rumors of my sexuality. It was my weakest point of attack when I was out there smoking crack and now ridicule for being gay in the environment of TeeLancey was causing just as much doom. Well; it wasn't going to happen so easily. The end of ten days had built up much anger and hatred due to the liability of my sexuality. At this third Games session began the same flow of remarks, straight out slander and defamation of my character. To defend myself with a civil tongue meant nothing to them therefore no possible win. Remarks of hatred toward especially my sexuality continued on from the first time until now in these so-called attack therapy sessions known as Games. Four letter words of the worst kind, of the most slanderous and degrading type poured from my mouth in rebuttal. The oral battle was on! The more I rebutted their remarks of hatred the more they poured it on. I had no win. But I felt a thousand percent better knowing I had given them a taste of their own poison. Consequently I forgot to take into consideration rules surrounding this play of Games. No physical violence of any kind (no body contact in anyway violent), no defaming or degrading such as the dozens and no speaking out of turn—you must raise your hand and be recognized by the team captain. These were rules I guess designed only for me. When the session opened I heard, for the first time, a woman say "I want to put the game on Nate" and as well she got recognized immediately by the team captain without her having raised her hand to be recognized. Wonder how she knew my name from the start? I was the star of the second and proceeding sessions. The first time was like being discovered and signed up for a contract in a movie to star as a faggot and center of ridicule. I paid attention or rather was very aware of the rules and how they were pretty much not adhered to. When I did violently rebut their constant ridicule it was of the worst kind without acknowledgement of it being the correct way to go about it or end such encounters not being cautious of the dozens I played right back at them as I called them names used like common language in the Tenderloin talking about their dearest family members. I even invited the same dude, who had been itching to see me busted, outside for a fight. I had even tried to get information about this therapy from the nurse and a fella who was to be a sort of counselor to me. I believe they called this kind of person a 'representative' for you in the program. He was the only one I could get a few minutes of conversation out of without hatred in his eyes and tone of voice. But I only met for the first time and talked with him one Friday night at an entertainment affair. I remember him advising me of TeeLancey Exit Recovery Program's tough program and being able to handle it. I wondered if other gays had been through the program and successfully completed it. I was called into that same room where I was interviewed to wait for the vice president of the program. Such found me soon in his office being yelled at about my ill participation in their so-called Games therapy. My asking him to please explain this therapy and if there was literature I could read on the philosophy of this kind of therapy produced an even louder tone telling me of my being put on probation and the next incident would be the end of TeeLancey Exit Recovery Program. Do they hate me that much? Guess this isn't for me. My self-respect can never be born again feeling like a lost, lonely, worthless reject. This is when I had begun to make up my mind to leave this program. There was just no win. Even the talk I had with the counselor seemed as if he was rushing and brushing me off as if he too was part of the gossip black balling me. After the reprimand and punishment I was in an awful frame of mind. I had been getting medication for my epilepsy condition from the nurse each night around 8:30. It was about half an hour after medication call upon leaving the vice president's office. I take Tegretol medication for epilepsy each night or the threat of a seizure especially in my sleep becomes very great. The nurse was nowhere to be found being as I was a half hour late for pill call. The reply from house management was that I should have taken time out to get my medication. How could I excuse myself from being reprimanded by the vice president? The nurse being unavailable and my being in an ill state of mind as well as tired from a long hard day made up the perfect ingredients to experience the seizure I suffered that night. As mentioned seizures occur most of the time in my sleep which is the reason for medication at bedtime. I tried to explain to house management my problem with epilepsy and the need for the medication. Nothing was done about it as if purposely neglected due to the hate that seemed to explode around me as I took a second look at the nightmare found this time without the help of crack cocaine. I went to bed without medication. This night of confusion, despair and depression over the outcome of the Games session caused this night in the dorms to erupt in a gran-mal seizure. This did not make matters any better or feelings toward me ease at all. It instead became worse. "If he wasn't gay he would not be a victim of epilepsy". After a seizure there are after effects of headache, bitten tongue and a disoriented feeling along with body aches from the engulfed muscle spasms. My disposition was now an even worse angered feeling set off by all that had happened. I was to move out of the dorm and back downstairs for what was said to be for my safety. My explaining or trying to explain to these people my being refused medication and why was simply ignored. I became so angry until I walked out the front door of this program with the return of a very familiar "I don't give a damn" attitude so use to during active addiction. A couple fellas followed me and talked me into coming back. I had no idea there were any people who may have really been good hearted and understanding enough to extend a compassionate hand needed so much in such a time of crisis. I came back with thoughts of hope rising from the words of strength from those two brothas. The word of my having left the program made it to the vice president's office just that fast. I wasn't gone five minutes. My departure really made their day until I came back with the fellas who had enough goodness in their hearts and souls to try and help—people I wished were found long ago in this program. Not only could there have been a positive attitude toward me but just maybe I would not have perpetuated myself to this point. It would also have kept me from violating a probation I may never have been put on. The return to TeeLancey Exit Recovery Program found me sitting on the intake bench once again feeling like a new intake only without having had one drop of crack in my system. I sat there knowing I would be told to leave; that I had violated my probation. But a chance in a million was what I hoped for. Where else could I go but back to the Tenderloin—back to The TL to GA and worst of all back to crack cocaine? It was only a few moments later I was told to depart TeeLancey Exit Recovery Program; that I had indeed violated the probation recently put on by walking out of the program in such a frustrated and emotional state of mind from all the negatives and ill thinking coming my way constantly from the beginning of this program. Tears began to flow once again to the thought of the TL and crack cocaine. Guess you can imagine the sorrow and emotional dilemma felt as I walked slowly out the door taking my last look at a place I thought really had promise to work for me upon entering its fresh attired atmosphere that first night as I witnessed all the happiness in such a pleasant environment. Little did I know that my chosen sexuality, even though not flaunted or implicated in anyway by my personality or actions, was indeed part of a prejudice in this program causing contempt, hatred and my not becoming the success I wanted to be. I remember Abe, the vice president, telling me of their having had gays in the program before. I don't recall his finishing that statement of those gays being success stories of TeeLancey Exit Recovery Program. All my hurt, shame and pity rested its weary body on a bench directly across the street from TeeLancey located at an entrance to Golden Gate Park. What to do now was a complicated question; one too massive for me to deal with. Thus the decision to lie down on a bench and rest my torn mental and emotional condition and find sleep was made. The beautiful blue sky, the mild breeze and warm sun put me to sleep on this bench I parked on that early afternoon. That evening sometime after seven I was wakened to the breeze having turned sharp and brisk, the sun having fallen but the day still full of daylight savings time. Coming from the windows of TeeLancey were sounds of the hell I experienced in their attack therapy better known as Games. My having fell so quickly into slumber was a definite indication of how mentally, emotionally and physically fatigued I was all due to what seemed the purposely induced seizure by TeeLancey the night before and the hard-head trip of hatred by people in what was supposed to be a help entity. Waking to the sound of cussing and venting of frustration along with being chilly from the wind and the sun's warmth having fallen behind the buildings to rest for the night found me in a continued angry mode. Going back to the Tenderloin was my only option which was a frightening thought. There I could probably muster up somewhere to lay my head for the night and simply pick up where I left off twelve days ago. GA checks were coming out soon so all I had to worry about were the three days until check day. That was good thinking after twelve days in TeeLancey spent not using. But my addiction had substituted hate for the check, a way I believe my addiction used to get me back to that scud missile which was a success. In fact my addiction had been totally successful at winning this battle after losing to my decision to find help with the first inpatient drug rehabilitation program ever tried. Thinking more about returning to the Tenderloin increased fear of going back and just as much increased anger for TeeLancey Exit Recovery Program for causing me to face what was the only choice to make besides going to prison. ***PRISON!!*** What a choice. It sounded like a resort hotel in Hawaii to me and was the answer to my problems—even better than the decision to try and turn myself in to police in order to get the needed help to stop using. In prison I could eat, rest and try something new—if positive entities existed in California's prison system as did the prison system in Washington State. My sexuality would certainly be much less of a problem than TeeLancey Exit Recovery Program even though it would cause me to become sexually active—a general factor of any prison's outline. I thought of the work I could do helping those achieve their levels in general education as was done in prison back home. There was the achievement of two associate degrees with a strong 'B' average, the discovery and work in art, braiding hair and making many more friends than those few enemies who hated me like those at TeeLancey. The prison system in California must surely be as good as, and even better than, my home state's prison system in Washington. As can probably be surmised I was or had found a perfect excuse to keep from further problems with crack by going back to prison. Maybe institutionalization was my real addiction, not the probable substituted nightmare of crack cocaine. Having done ten years over two sentences over a fourteen year period back home caused my institutionalized thinking to react in what I thought was a solution to the sorrow and bleak situation I was in. I had made up my mind to return to prison. How to do it was the next question which was followed by quick reaction. Upon focusing back into the Games that could still be heard very clear from across the street where I sat came the anger revitalizing itself to full peak. Looking and scanning the building I noticed the dumpster in the parking lot on the side of the building. I had dumped their garbage and knew that routine. Arson came into full focus as I thought of the cart full of broken down cardboard boxes next to the dumpster. I remember the night during my wanting to be arrested at the city jail again due to the nightmare of crack and how I set numerous dumpsters on fire. This must be where I got this idea. Little did I know I was probably psychologically ill with arson behavior. Crack! What a way to bring out hidden negatives. Even worse I can't recall anything positive crack has ever brought out of me. The crack rap was a force in me fighting the crack monster. I had matches and even a few bucks. I went to the store around the corner and bought a couple candy bars as I was very hungry and a can of charcoal starter fluid. It did not start the fire as I wanted the effect to be. After a few matches here and there in the dumpsters I rolled it against the wall alongside the cart full of cardboard. A few more matches on the broken down cardboard began a small flame and very little smoke. During this time my nerves were completely shot. If someone had caught me and yelled out in defense of the building's safety I would probably have collapsed. I was more scared then I could ever remember. It is funny because this and just a few other crimes out of the many are the only crimes of such magnitude I ever remember. All the crimes back home except for one are lost in memory. Maybe this is good. The only one I remember back home is an assault because it had great merit on my family life. Looking back on setting that fire to or rather the entire experience of TeeLancey Exit Recovery Program saw how diseased I actively was in addiction. By the same token I see now how hard a battle I fought even though I was losing most of these encounters in battle even after the victory night sitting on the intake bench of TeeLancey. Here I was twelve days later fighting even harder. The fire had been set and the very small flames were enough for me as I hastened a very quick retreat back to the same bench area across the street in the park. It took some minutes but soon there began a thick cloud of smoke pouring into the open windows over and around the dumpster now flaming at a progressive height. The cart with its cardboard began to burn with the same perpetuation. A couple minutes into the high flames and smoke saw the interruption of Games and the evacuation of the building. The sirens of fire trucks were heard as they quickly approached to put out what was only a small fire—but a fire large enough to be considered arson by law and my ticket to hopeful freedom from the pure hell suffered up to that very instant. As mentioned setting the fire caused my frightened paranoid condition to enhance almost as much as the peak of the many crack cocaine episodes smoking alone. I could not come out of the forest area in the park and go across the street to turn myself in. How was I going to get arrested? Thus I waited there under the cover of the trees in the park hoping the police or firemen would come and get me. My wish did not come true and it was there I waited now more confused and scared than before. Night had fallen only an hour or so later and I became more courageous about my determination to get arrested. I set two more fires this time on the opposite side of the TeeLancey building in their porch area. It only smoldered and the smoke penetrated through the door seams on the porch. Around eleven o'clock that night I began preparing the third and final fire. I was caught by one of the residents in the program who had been planted. I had built up enough courage this time upon his catching me set another fire. I did not do what I knew would have happened in this instance during the first fire. Instead I was frightened by his surprising me but still I told him to call the police. I told him how I was the one causing the fires and I would continue to do so until the police took me to jail. I told him I was not going back to the Tenderloin and how prison was a much better alternative chosen over the pains and pure hell of addiction in the worst area of the city—the only part of the city I knew to go after being ousted from TeeLancey Exit Recovery Program. One thing I noticed about successful residents of a year or more in this program is how they seem to have hard attitudes and feelings. Their emotions and thought kind of processes we all have seem altered by what may be the attack therapy's breaking down of the individual and rebuilding a new person free of drugs. To say that something like this is indeed fact would be wrong on my part. Remember I am diseased and unlike that successful majority in this program they are drug free today. My own excuse seeking and vengeful thinking could very well be a misinterpretation. Having been busted by this resident of

TeeLancey I was told to vacate the area and not to return. Again there was no call to police for my arrest. What made confusion and dismay even worse for me was my calling 911 and telling the lady operator how I had tried to set the program on fire. I told her where I was and I would be at this phone booth waiting arrival of authorities. But she took this as a prank call and hung up. This gave me all the reason and right in the world to set more fires around the area not far from TeeLancey. Like excuse seeking for drugs I had substituted arson this night for drugs as was done the night arrested for vandalism. What a way to express one's body and mind pleading and bleeding ills. But then a war was going on. I wanted an answer to problems addiction fought so hard to keep from me. These were ways I fought the addict in me. In this area about six blocks from TeeLancey I began setting fires to dumpsters and piles of trash. There was a wood frame construction site I set fire to but was put out by someone in a pub just across the street. Walking around feeling like a lost spaceship in the endless and vast outer-limits of space with tears again found in my eyes, representing the condition of a weary mind, body and soul confused and in emotional despair led me to a grassy area a block from TeeLancey Exit Recovery Program where I laid down and found almost immediate slumber despite the cold in the air. Time was in the very early AM around two or three o'clock. It was very chilly at forty or so degrees. I had no warm clothing to fight off the chill. As well it was a cold and misty rainy night the time before when experiencing setting fires to dumpsters around the city's jail. Maybe that was the psychological reasoning behind all the fires. Daybreak woke me to the sun beaming down on me. I started the walk to the dreaded TL—the place I did not want to return. It was early enough to make the hotline and it was there on Otis Street I found shelter and where another ten days in the Tenderloin found me experiencing the recycled madness of addiction before finally be taken or rather taking myself off the streets and in the prison system away from the physical horror of crack cocaine—something I wanted to happen immediately following the end of TeeLanceyt Street. Hotline paid off with a hotel room outside the TL which may have been a good idea except my addiction had won all the battles while in TeeLancey getting me ousted and winning the battle that night keeping me from being arrested and finally installing more anger, fear and hatred along with self-pity, sorrow and the like so that I could be ready for the GA check. The achievement of a hotline room at a hotel just off Polk out of the TL was where I waited out the remaining day to receive the final GA check and go on the final run with crack cocaine before being given the break from the madness I suffered. Physical madness was relieved but later told of emotional and mental feelings still being actively addicted and progressing with even more assurance of continued use. I remember how well I slept the night before picking up my check. I recall the sun still shining brightly the morning of August 1st. However I recall very little until the 7th of August on the night before I turned myself into authorities due to TeeLancey finally having given my name as the suspected cause of the fires at their site. Remembering very little include one night sleeping at a shelter in a church on Gough Street near the receptionist job I held during the first run I experienced in the city. I ate at an old fire station site down by the piers on Third Street used to feed the homeless. I had met a man, JM, whose sobriety covered some ten years. I knew he wanted to be my sponsor but I, the one in need, had to ask him to be such. I was not ready for a sponsor to help me in my quest for what was only sobriety at that time although we talked about recovery prior to this during times I sought help and my involvement with the coalition. I ran into him just after the first and we talked about TeeLancey Exit Recovery Program and how it had left me with a confused and angered mind. He helped me out with emergency shelter at the Donation center's shelter program (Sally) in the TL on Eddy Street. He mentioned my trying an in-house program of another nature not like the outline of attack therapy prescribed by TeeLancey. I tried to pursue the farm at the catholic organization around the corner from Great Tide church—the one feeding homeless all they can eat each day in the two hours they were open to them. I applied and got a letter from Sally of recommendation and their attesting to my clean and sober condition during the five days I was there. There were a number of times during homelessness in the TL I stayed at Sally's shelter. As well it is talked about very highly by all. 'Bologna Bingo' wins you an extra sandwich if your bed number is called. This is very welcomed when coming in the shelter the first night from a crack run or whatever nightmare. Showers are a must before being given PJs, linen and a bed. The operation used at this shelter seems designed to keep confusion to a very low minimum. It was on the sixth day of August that I was turned down for the farm at the location of the other main TL feeding site. There was no reason given for my not being a good candidate for their farm. Just that my application was turned down. What was a bit shocking for me was finding out that the intake counselor of this organization, who gave me the news of my not being accepted for this program, was and may still be actively using crack. What an accusation; but a true one. With a surprise urine test this would prove to be true provided this person is not already too far lost in addiction having given up his position at this foundation in the TL. The shock was my purchasing crack only two days later and seeing this intake counselor purchasing his own problems with addiction. Food stamps were picked up the next day and I sold them for the usual 65 dollars. I went back to the Hostility House where I had been hanging out to see if a guy name Chuck was still there. I had been playing spades with him and told him that I would get him high if I got and sold my food stamps. He was there and he had a hotel room in the sixth and Mission area—the same block of the Shelta. He knew where to cop and we used his room. The highlight of this night was my taking a hit of crack and feeling a wild sensation as if my body was shaking like never before. I raved about how good this dope was and wanted to spend the remaining thirty bucks on more of it. To my dismay it was that day, at that time San Francisco had experienced the first of two earthquakes. This one was not nearly as big as the October earthquake that followed but enough to feel its penetration. I began a tweeked out affair with Chuck that led to those ugly thoughts of depression, remorse, more self-pity and the usual. The cycle of the high had again met with the same exact circumstances and its endings. I began to think about the program at TeeLancey and how I had not made it a success. My depression became more involved. Having tried to put myself away in jail to escape the same feelings and continued nightmare with crack was a foremost thought that prompted me to find out if in fact my name had come up as a suspect of the fire at TeeLancey Exit Recovery Program. I figured that a police report of some kind would have to be made due to the responded call of firemen who put out the fire. It was about a week and a half now. If I had a warrant or whatever, I could find out through my probation officer. And it was that I had a warrant out for my arrest. Guess it may sound sick to many of you who still use and think you have it together and in fact may have good connections and lots of cash; but I was so relieved and full of joy to find out there was a way out of the bottom of that last hit for so many, many times. My probation officer and I talked over the phone and she gave me the Lt. Investigator's name and number. I told her of all that had happened and how crack was a much bigger problem than I had come to realize until TeeLancey Exit Recovery Program. I knew not getting arrested from this program meant going back to the only part of town and life I knew at that time. She wished me luck and we parted over the phone. I never saw her again. As soon as I hung up with this call I didn't even hang the receiver up. I dropped another quarter in the phone and contacted this Lt. Investigator.

He was in and the search for me was a process that took no time to complete. Briefly we talked about what had happened and I told him I would be right down. Upon arriving we talked more in-depth about TeeLancey and my stay there. After the conversation and such he put me under arrest but only put the cuff s on me for formalities sake. He knew I was not going to run. I wanted off the streets of San Francisco. It took sometime but I accomplished what soon came—prison and the physical clean and sober time I needed. This officer mentioned that a recommendation from him of my having turned myself in and my desire for recovery would reach whatever judge I went before. I didn't think such a small, potentially drastic fire could bring me a sixteen year sentence recommended by the prosecutor. But the judge expressed his concern and knowledge of a crime done out of passion and his compassion found me being sentenced to sixteen months in prison where I could use the time to clean up and find clean thoughts a vehicle to find a life in recovery. Thus; this is the story of a drug program that is not, by any means, geared for just anybody wanting freedom from the traps of addiction. Seems to me it takes a special class of people who fit the category of such a philosophy spelled out in the attack therapy used to build a new person free of drugs. A gay man or woman may take this story for what it is worth in deciding on a program to get clean in. If you need the breaking down of the person you hate that lives inside you and being born again into a new human free of life prior to and including drugs and need it done in a demeaning way then TeeLancey Exit Recovery Program is your ticket to a new you. But as mentioned during the twelve day stay there I noticed those well into the program and those success stories of the program that seem to have hardnosed attitudes. Maybe it was just the turned cheek toward me due to my sexual preference. Whatever the case at this program I cannot nor will I ever submit to the degradation of what was felt so intensely to be a show of hate due to my being gay. They were not doctors of psychology. They were all addicts just like me. Who were they to judge my being gay as the one and only cause of my addiction? Who gives such a program the right to judge in this fashion? Yes; sex is directly related to the crack high and frustration of its accomplishment due to the psychological pattern of the high that continues to intensify the addiction and the search for sex. But if I were straight and searching only for female, heterosexual sex, would there be any difference in intensity for a female sex partner to accompany the crack, wine and candlelight?

CENTURIES LATER

WHY IS THE SALE OF ALCOHOLIC BEVERAGES;
ALSO NOT MADE ILLEGAL AS IS THE USE OF
DRUGS WITH ITS ADDICTING DAMAGES?

AGAIN AMERICA SHOWS ANOTHER INBALANCE
SEEN IN OTHER AREAS OF LIFE SUCH AS
SEGREGATION'S HARD CALLUS
OR THOSE LIVING IN THEIR
MILLION DOLLAR PALACE
NOT GIVING A DAMN ABOUT HOMELESS
JANIS, ALICE OR ALEX

YAH! I SAID IT! SEGREGATION!!
A WAY TO KEEP UP THE CONTINUED FRUSTRATION
MONITORED LIKE STOCK IN THE WAREHOUSES
OF AMERICA'S POVERTY STRICKEN NATION
WHERE LIFE CARRIES ON WITH
PROGRESSING DEGREGATION
MAINTAINING AND BREEDING YEARS
OF LOW CLASS GENERATIONS

AND INSTEAD OF LEARNING THE AMMUNITION
OF TECHNOLOGY AND PSYCHOLOGY
THERE IS CONTINUED DROPPING OUT OF MIDDLE
SCHOOL ONLY TO ENHANCE THE FORMATION
AND FRUSTRATION OF 'GANGOLOGY'
AND ITS GANG COLONIES
YO MAN! HATE TO SOUND LIKE A REPEAT-
QUACK BUT WHAT'S UP WITH DAT!!!
GETTIN' TIRED OF BEING TAKEN BACK
YAH! IT WAS EASY ACHIEVIN' A DRINK, A
HEAD FULLA PCP AND/OR CRACK
FOR THAT ONE MOMENT WE WAS HELLA FAT
AGAIN AND AGAIN LIFE TAKES CONTROL
AND STEPS ON US LIKE A DOE MAT WONDER
IF AT 13 PLUS YEARS OLD IS ANYONE READY
TO MAKE TO MAKE A REAL COMBACK?
DON'T KNOW 'BOUT YA' BUT I'M GETTIN'
THE HELL OUTTA THIS DAMN SHACK!
YA'LL DOWN AT WELFARE AND IN THE STREETS
OF NOWHERE CAN KEEP YO YACKETY YACK
CAUSE I AIN'T GONNA BE PART OF THAT
CENTURIES OLD, WITH NO BENEFITS
ATTACHED, FAKE CONTRACT
AND THAT MY YOUNG BROTHAS AND
SISTAS WHO ARE TO BECOME TOMORROW'S
LEADERS, IS STRAIGHT UP FACT!!!

V

Recovery In Prison?

Having been sentenced to sixteen months in prison and off the streets, especially out of the Tenderloin (TL), was a time to mentally prepare myself for prison for a third time in my life. My reason for choosing prison, as mentioned, was due to having become institutionalized over the past fifteen years with two prior stretches in prison and lots of jail time. Prison at home was an exciting new experience which achieved for me an education from my GED to and including two associate degrees. Prison back home also opened up the discovery for visual arts. It was mentioned that had I matured the discovery for the arts at a much earlier time in life I may have become something other than an addict. Social groups of all types to aspire to and meet productive people working toward a new life and who respected my progress in school were all right there behind the walls of prison. Add to this the many brothas' hair I braided, both corn row and French, making me one of the most sought after hair stylist on the yard. Being gay in prison was something I could easily deal with. I neither hated nor loved the gay life in prison. There is much more to this reasoning and its evaluation as a gay man in prison than I will reveal at this time. But many convicts seek the company of gays behind bars for obvious reason. Washington State's prison system was a plus for me because of knowing many of the brothas' populating prison. I remember many people as far back as grade school. Many knew of my being gay long before prison and others knowing members of my small family which made my popularity and my goals achieved in school and the arts an even greater plus for me. All in all prison back home was a very good and rewarding experience which led to my decision to do a stretch in the penal system of California. Desires I thought would help achieve me sturdy ground after prison including more education, tutoring and writing. But the dismay in prison I was sentenced to did all but inspire a new life for me or inspire any positive thoughts leading to the success I tried to work on but had no success achieving. My mental pattern was deterred greatly. The California prison system had basically the same working mechanics: a prison full of convicts, a yard to socialize, exercise and run track in, cell blocks housing from one to eight convicts to a cell (larger than back home), outside social groups such as the No Namedsociety, church, clothing and linen to exchange on a scheduled basis, guards better known as 'turn-keys' who issue infraction reports (write-ups) and count convicts a number of times each day, in-house recreation areas for watching TV, playing cards, ping pong, chess and dominoes, and gun towers, wall and control stations that watch for escapes. All these parts generally make up the basic prison. But I made the decision to again become incarcerated. As stated prison back home was a very positive experience for me. The work in school and all other experiences, more good than bad, gave me the outlet needed to begin the long assessment road for a better life. Without having achieved this much I would be in much worse shape with an addiction than I could imagine what with being ignorant to add to a suborn addiction as well. The social entity back home was full of everyday social activities. Positive outside people and organizations visited the prison daily. A whole floor in the prison's social building is complete with cultural, ethnic and general services to become involved in. Dances, graduation from the college program, weddings in the chapel and the like kept me in contact with society and good spirit in school. Hard work to accomplish my goals in school along with fellow residents and friends rooting for me were part of this positive experience in prison back home. Thus it was that I got sentenced to sixteen months and sent to a facility in Susanville, California. It is interesting to note too that the judge, it seems, only prescribed sixteen months instead of sentencing me to what could have been up to sixteen years in prison. It is simple to figure out that with the basics of any prison system there is with each prison a unique environment. My first look at the California prison system was a Prison reception center in a section of the prison called West Block. It is a receiving unit where almost all of California's incoming convicts come to be classified for one of the more than twenty-five prison facilities in the state as is the Shelton facility back home. This is at least a four week stay. This cell block is where I got the first taste of the poorly operated prison system in California—probably due to the many more convicts populating prisons than my home in Washington. Here is where I formulated an opinion of the prison system in California. It is truly not what I expected having done so much time back home. Of course prison I guess is not supposed to be a place where one can get a new start in life—a positive one anyway. Guess maybe a few have and therefore it can be the fight and the struggle added to the already existing problems of incarceration allowing one to come out a winner without the infection of institutionalization—the biggest problem. This was not the case for me though. The first instance of a prison that began the daily thoughts and forming of opinions was when I saw signs of pure warehousing and excessive recidivism. This also perpetuated institutionalization, hatred, prejudices and the like. I also found such to be the case in the medical department. If you recall I am an epileptic. My particular disorder finds seizures occurring predominately during slumber as opposed to waking hours. I remember few seizures occurring during waking hours since having been diagnosed with this medical condition. This has been going on for close to fifteen years now. Epilepsy has no known cure but the seizures are controlled by the doctor prescribed medication. Here is where I question the system's promise and/or practice of good care that is supposed to make up the California prison medical department. There is the required format of physicals for each new and returning convict and is when and where epilepsy was made known to their health department and treated. By the same token the West Block itself filters a huge volume of convicts in and out of their reception facility almost daily. Add to this the amount of convicts going and coming that make up the cry of overcrowded prisons in this state. Transferring, shipping and receiving has thus become termed "a business" where convicts are classed as cattle or livestock in route to the more than twenty-five grazing lands and butcher shops located throughout the state. How accurate and well operated is the hospital let alone any other entity in this system at West Block what with all the incoming and outgoing convicts? All of them must go through the health department of this facility. The amount of patients flowing through their small hospital on a constant basis seems an interesting figure to allow for standard judging of such a facility. Is each and every convict cared for with the standard expertise needed every hour and many times minute and second of the day? If I were to suffer a seizure would I be rushed to the infirmary as quickly and as professionally as are those emergency entities in the so-called free world? If I were to go into a seizure because of prison guard brutality which ended up in their carting me off to detention instead of the infirmary due to lack of medical training and its rescue knowledge of such a condition; would the waking result still get me treated for the after effects of a gran-mal seizure? Or would the truth have to be hidden in order to escape a law suit? Such was the case during the first sentence served back home in Washington State (1970s) in their much smaller more adequate prison system (7 prisons in Washington State compared to 25 in California). Does an overcrowded situation in prison interrupt the flow of excellent care provided each convict by highly paid and quality hospital staff as are those at General Hospitals in San Francisco? Maybe the term convict is a reason these questions come about. Seems that paying a debt to society does not or may not adhere to the promise of medical care for a law breaker what with so many perfect citizens out there voting the fate of new prisons and its operation (death penalty). Deserving convicts may be a bit much to focus on right now. But what about a convict who falls off the top bunk in a prison cell from a seizure? To be assigned a top bunk knowing I am an epileptic is just another of the many miscalculations in a place like prison. But to be negligent in dispensing proper medication to guard against the sure eruption of gran-mal seizures caused me to suffer an even greater misfortune in California's prison system. Bear with me through a total of twelve months in the California prison system as it had significant merit on my outcome. Several seizures occurred while at the reception center in the west block area of this prison I was classified for and sent to. Medical care for the treatment of epilepsy was a problem I faced from the beginning until my release on parole from Susanville. It was a two month stay in San Quentin's prison reception center before being shipped out to Susanville prison (Susie's House) in October 1989. Upon arriving at the reception center I was assigned the first of several top bunks potentially hazardous to my health and safety as an epileptic. There is a classification process each convict must go through before being selected and shipped to whatever prison. While in the first assigned cell, 2-west-79, I suffered the first of several seizures due to improper medical care. I had been to what is known as 'sick-call' and informed the infirmary of my need for seizure medication. The need for medication was not fulfilled until I suffered a seizure less than a week after arriving. I informed them of the need to be assigned a bottom bunk due to the danger of falling from a top bunk during a seizure. Luckily I did not fall from the top bunk in the first cell. Consequently I was assigned a different cell, 1-west-98, on the first tier. I believe communication was somehow not completely read or it was misunderstood because I was again assigned to the top bunk in this second cell. It is my belief the order was interpreted wrong. I notified the infirmary through in-house mail or memo known as a 'kite'. No word of my sending a kite was responded to nor was I moved to a bottom bunk. I was very concerned about this because of the prior seizure and the very possible chance of falling off that top bunk. I was very concerned because of the infirmary lacking responsibility to insure my getting seizure control medication—not a fix! Seems I had to have a seizure in order to be properly attended to for my seizure disorder. Again after the move to the first tier I was forgotten about somehow and medication not dispensed. If the Tegretol medication is not taken nightly the chance of a seizure within 36 hours, usually during the next night's sleep, is very great. It had been a couple of days of written memos (kites) to the infirmary as well as going to sick-call to inform them my need for medication. I was fortunate not to suffer a seizure right away. But a seizure finally occurred a few days later on an afternoon while I slept and I was rushed to their so-called infirmary. This time I fell from the top bunk. The cellie I shared this cell with was quick in helping me get to the infirmary with his call for help and getting me back in the top bunk. He was new on what to do in such a situation where seizures are involved. But he was quick to act and I appreciated it very much upon finding out thereafter. After more expressing about the need to put me on a bottom bunk and to make sure I had medication directly vital in controlling the problem of seizures occurring, I was moved from

1-west-98 to 1-west-63. This cell lasted about as long as it took to move my mattress and bedding before being told this particular cell was in reserve for another convict with epilepsy—likely story! Overcrowding in prison had truly out-done itself with that bit of news. The final assignment at the West Block was just two cells away in 1-west-65 where I completed the 57 day stay at this reception center with a very attractive gang member who made the sexual desire apart of my homosexuality come alive and caused me to forget about my disorder. I was classified for Susanville about five days later. Communication between the infirmary to the West Block was a definite problem. I was not assigned to a bottom bunk at all except for the one cell already assigned to another epileptic. There is more to this incarceration than just the misfortune of my not receiving proper medical treatment for my disorder even though this went on throughout the entire sentence served in California's Correctional System. What is more interesting to maybe look at was how this system seems to be a business enterprise with recidivism a major commodity. This seems to be the reason such medical care lacked in importance to them. I cannot personally give numbers or percentages. What I can say is what I personally experienced. Overcrowding is aired on television's talk shows, commentaries, news and the like here in California and probably all of America—especially the many in jails. But the business of overcrowding seems translated into many dollars for many people in the business of operating the many jails and prisons. Recycling convicts may be the number one commodity in the more than twenty-five prison sites in California. What are the possible reasons behind both recidivism and overcrowding? I have heard negative responses held by many. To focus on better thinking and to get away from so much existing hatred on both sides of this controversy of prison the question of what is in prison for the convict to aspire to should be evaluated and how overcrowding and detouring crime is possibly being dealt with. To compare the

Washington state prison system to the one here in California is my own opinion. I saw very little to aspire to in Susanville. Yes; there was education but for someone with two associate degrees eager to help those students striving for the same GED I struggled through in the same kind of environment, I got nowhere fast. There was no positive atmosphere for a convict to go and talk to another convict or social worker (counselor) in the prison like the social floor in Washington State or the education center behind gate seven away from the general atmosphere of prison. There was the usual complicated formality that is very discouraging for someone who may want an answer that could very well change his or her life behind bars. To attend a GED class at Monroe's Reformatory back home was a simple yellow kite put in a request/kite box and that convict's name/number appearing on a clearance sheet within three days to see the education facility staff. If he was serious and wanted to give it a try he began work in the GED lab where the head teacher, a couple of college interns along with student convicts taking accelerated classes all worked with the new student. I spent eighteen months of a six and a half year sentence toiling for my GED. It was a fight so well worth the battle. It was enhanced by the college program having a full course for degree achievement. I paroled with a two year associate degree in Art & Science. Add to this a grade point average (GPA) of 3.3 putting me on the honor's role. I really thought I could share my knowledge with others in the school program at the prison I was in here in California. But my desire to become part of the school program on a peer level/tutor basis was denied. No response from the requests to be part of the word-processing department of education was responded to as well. A couple visits and demonstrated ability to be an asset to the education department seemed rejected by the employed teaching staff. Their answer to my wanting to be part of the education team was their not having such a program for convicts to aspire to. There was no college for me to advance my own education which was a letdown—not even by mail. Seems I was shunned instead of welcomed to possible opportunity I could work and strive for as done in prison back home. To push my way into the education department would probably cause me more grief than reward. My sexuality was enough to deal with even though my rapport in school would have been straight up with any student seeking serious help. Maybe that is why they shunned me. Nobody really knew I was gay until I was approached by some old TL Tossup from the past. An example of the kind of rapport I kept with a student of mine was while I was in the hole (segregation). Out of a dozen or so cellmates during the six months I was in this section, at least four of them sought basic educational help from me of some kind—if not just to see a mind at work—a rarity for many in prison. Having a good enough basic education can amaze those drop-outs who haven't seriously thought of furthering themselves. Some were very serious and one, my favorite, was a student attempting his GED. His name was Louisiana. Math has always been a favorite subject of mine and he wanted to advance in it. When I finally got to fractions and percentages with Louisiana I knew I had made a good friend. His being a gang member and in his thirties now made me feel confident about him. Two others were gang members who were pretty hard to deal with but wanted and sought knowledge they saw in me. My sexuality kept them in the right frame of mind; believe it or not, with a cool and collected enough pattern of thought for me to get their questions answered and feed them the right knowledge in academics that got me my GED. Keep in mind that being gay in prison is nothing new and in fact is a well-accepted part of prison life by the majority. But such can be hard on gays. Spreading oneself around and letting the atmosphere of being surrounded by men become a fantasy world will create problems. These men, most of them, are heterosexual not bisexual and certainly not totally gay (homosexual). Their need for sexual satisfaction and feminine company has allowed gays to be an accepted part of prison for, I guess, as long as there have been such closed environments separating man from his woman. Being from a place like the TL did not help matters at all because there were those who I had smoked with and tossed-up. This got the word of my sexuality out from almost the very beginning of the almost one year spent in Susie's House. To deny my being gay would only complicate my doing time in such an environment. There would be those doing their best to kick me out of a closet I was not in. There were difficult enough times in prison to deal with to have to bear this ridicule. From both sides I saw difficulty in achieving a positive program, one that would let me find peace of mind and a sense of accomplishment allowing the kind of thought pattern needed in hopefully dealing with my addiction. From the beginning at the reception center in San Quentin I was asked for sexual favors. Playing smart led me to becoming cellmates with as few as possible who had status enough to keep respect in enough focus for me. In a prison setting if the gay gets celled up with one who is well known and 'tough' there is much less trouble to deal with. Thus respect is having status in the iron pile (weight lifters) and being a fighter having busted ground through victorious fights in the prison's boxing ring or even a fatal incident known throughout. This also keeps threats of spreading oneself around and its possible ramifications to a limit. But doing this takes a little picking and choosing which can be and was dangerous for me. Details of the initial encounter in Susie's House are of much embarrassment and shame. Some terrible things happened including being jumped on, ridiculed, put in detention and segregated due to having carried syphilis into prison with me causing me to be involved with the wrong situation and its people in a prison setting I did not foresee. Because the education department was not a place I could become involved in I found myself on what is known as the yard crew. A rake, shovel or a broom and plastic sack were tools used to keep the yard as clean as possible for the population to continue its school of criminology. The major function aside from cards, dominoes, chess, the iron pile and handball is the idle talk among each other consisting mainly of war stories of the streets. Gays also braid hair of which I again became known for. Thus if one hangs around long enough one day he becomes a student of crime. Church and limited outside social groups are treated more like privileges that must be earned with good work reports and so on. Attitudes held by many guards are very backward and what seems KKK orientated. Wow! What is the mental capacity of a correctional officer in the south? To be a prison guard takes a high school diploma or GED, no arrest record and a number of weeks training—Hah? After all, one only need the knowledge of counting accurately, turning keys and watching out for escape attempts. Writing the convict up (infraction report) and verbally reprimanding convicts are included in this kind of career along with being fit enough to handle the breaking up of fights or whatever and carting those off to the 'hole'. At times there are correctional officers who impose their authority on convicts for unjust reason. If prison correctional officers were investigated the probable show of a tremendous or at least more than average volume of alcoholism may indeed arise. This is so because of the interaction of COs talking about their days off on the job at their favorite pub and how many times they "tied-one-on". Counselors are a mystery at this prison. I do not remember my assigned counselor's name or names as I was moved around quite a lot during my short sentence. Developing a relationship or some type of rapport with someone in such a position was not possible for me to achieve. I had not given my Higher Power the chance needed back then which kept me from trying the chapel. In fact I was rather frightened of this entity. I know this feeling was not a unique one. Excuse seeking sought ill rationalizing which lured me from the only other positive entity in prison aside from education— God. Having been transferred from yard to yard, put in segregation and suffering continued improper medical treatment for my epilepsy along with other factors deterred any logical thinking about what to do to make at least sobriety a permanent part of my life and its future outside of prison. The main theme or finale of all the war stories was crack cocaine. To elaborate further with Susie's House story it wasn't long, less than two months, during incarceration that the picking and choosing got me in trouble for homosexual conduct causing some complications. I was glad to be put in segregation/detention for some weeks before finally being put on another yard populated by more mature and older convicts. Maybe they should have put me, a 38 year old repeat off ender from another state in with those in my age group having done time already instead of a yard full of gladiators. I was a first timer in their state prison system but not for the first time behind prison walls. The end result was my refusing to go back to this yard and having to wait a number of months, close to the end of my sentence, before being classified for the three yard. The three yard was the only one of the three with at least an older norm to have to deal with—ole'timers. While doing time in segregation I had a number of cellmates. These were the dozen or so mentioned earlier having enjoyed tutoring a few of them. I waited over a month before getting sexually involved again due to the medical problem of syphilis. Seems after the symptoms and sickness of this disease it was told how it is a permanent part of my blood system and how I can still infect or pass this disease on. Sex was something I could not escape even in the hole even if I wanted to refrain from it. So to keep from having a new cellie week after week I finally gave in to WR. This dude was gang affiliated and had his eye on me from day one in the hole. When I was moved to the section of the hole he was in he began pitching his need for a cellie—or in my case a "Blade". Such is a gay boy celled up with his 'daddy'. He knew I braided hair and began purchasing my time on his hair. I began to like his friendliness. We laughed, joked and he as well needed and wanted academic help he knew I possessed. I wrote letters to family and friends for him, read his mail to him and finally said yes to his constant pressure to move with him. I had also decided it was not a bad idea at all because I had grown to like WR. His friendliness convinced me even more along with his high status as a gang member—a commander. Having never been involved in the gangs of today except to buy their crack, I knew very little about them. Over the time celled with a gangster I came to know the thinking process and actions of someone like WR. He became attached very quickly. Braiding his hair, keeping our cell clean (he liked to clean as well), writing letters for him, tutoring him, conversation with him and basically representing him as his 'blade' which of course included sex all made time a bit easier to do for the short time this pattern of our relationship lasted. After about six weeks of our affair came demands, frustration and especially the continued progressive lustful sex. I don't think dude was 100 percent heterosexual. WR demanded sex every night which was the main factor that spoiled the relationship between us. With this came his becoming more and more attached. The way he involved himself each night in the act of sex could hardly be called love or normal heterosexual lust. He was acting out his fantasy for his women out on me—something definitely not unusual; but every night? I was a scapegoat for the passions of the women in Oakland where he is from of which he raved and constantly talked about. He told stories of murders, the near million made selling dope and how he worked the hard road to his commander status in his chosen gang in Oakland. The women in his dreams caused him to stay oversexed therefore taking his fantasies out on me. It was obvious that all the stories of his gangster life were a life he loved dearly. Before moving with him I was led to believe his life as a gangster would be interesting to hear all about. Talking about it while braiding his hair twice a week made it sound even more exciting. The fact that he knew a major million dollar dope dealer in Oakland, that people knew of and talked about way back home in Seattle, may have been a main highlight from my wanting to hear his entire gangster background. Another factor I considered very strongly was his age. At thirty-four I just knew the maturity element involved in a potential prison relationship would work. I was only five years his senior which made our ages pretty compatible. Little did I know our ages were no match compared to years of his violence, selling dope, the brothahood between the gangster-hood he loved and being raised in Oakland, California. WR was, at thirty-four, five feet nine maybe ten inches tall, approximately 160 pounds, with a deep rich and rough caramel complexion, brown eyes, black hair and a rough fast talking voice. His voice isn't scratchy but instead rough and very sexy matching his rough complexion. He had a very friendly personality so unusual about him. He had no trouble winning a friendship and the hearts of women. His fear is locked in the violence of this new age gangster era that distracts the wonderful person he really is. Guess you could say I felt a lot for WR. He let go much of his better qualities and feelings through his emotions expressed in our solitude aside from sex. His mother is a very well to do woman who worked hard to get the higher class position she had living in Oakland. WR's rearing being in this state in the city of Oakland has afforded him the status of many friends and his well-known cultured environment in an Oakland gang affiliation that will never be known to anyone because of the feelings I guess I'll forever hold for him. Bad times, though, began to sprout after the initial 'honeymoon', to be humorous, was over. I became worn out from the sex and wanted to cut it down. I began showing signs that were picked up as rejection. He began ego-tripping' with violent oral rebuttals. Instead of scaring me he began to do something to the affair that spoiled it. These rebuttals were only oral at first but over a period of weeks near the end there were a few incidents where he physically put strain on me—something I thought he would not do. He never socked me nor beat me down in a straight out way. He did not want to hurt me and I knew this. Be advised that because he was smaller than me he did in fact have just as much status and respect in the iron pile and among his gangster peers. This factor shined through his tight, hard, very cut and shaped rugged body from chest to toes. He was a very strong, obviously masculine man. As well he was ruggedly handsome. One of the incidents where he got so frustrated and so mad at me was his grabbing me by the neck and choking me in sequential order a few times and telling me how he hated me. This was due to my having made up excuses not to have sex with him that lasted over a week. So it was that he had been too intense with sex and I was not in condition to withstand the constant pressure of his lustful desires. But during this week or nine days I had completely healed from the constant banging sex that caused so much uncomfortable pressure. And by this time I had developed great desire for WR and wanted to work our way through this tender time and its lust. But I was afraid, too shamed—I don't really know. I just couldn't tell him. It wasn't until after this choking incident that I could see he cared for me in a very weird way and I was able to tell him what was on my mind. This must have been the highlight of our relationship because I instead became the deviant sexual monster who began lusting sexually for him. It never occurred to me how much he had been talking and promising me our encounter in Oakland, that his women knew of his sexual desires in prison, that not just any faggot could spark his fancy, that because he loved to have sex constantly was not the only reason he wished my company or companionship and that our relationship had grown into something more than what I thought it was. It then came to me how women and feminine genders can become addicted to pain and get into Sadomasochism (S & M) because of how he did not want to hurt me but get my attention through such intense masculine lustful tactics used to express a very urgently needed message to me. I am the one who became infested with sexual desired for him. The turnabout was crazy fair play because I began attacking him each night without fail which puzzled him. This was nothing he could not get over but he was not sure of me from that time on. No; this was not a psychological tactic used as I knew very little if nothing at all of such therapy. Something else I remember very clearly was his telling me he did not smoke cocaine. He only sold it. This is where I began to believe whole heartedly the stories of coming so close to a net profit of a million dollars. I recall how he kept insisting upon my not smoking crack and that I would be his worst enemy/nightmare compared to his best friend if he ever saw someone he cared about out there full of the shit. He would make an attempt to clean me up by putting me in one of those detox or whatever programs and extend his love; but if it did not work it was "see ya' later" and depending on his mood he would take me out of my misery or dump me forever letting me live to suffer the awesome addiction. He said he would even put a quarter pound in my hands with such a goodbye knowing what effects it would have on me. He knows as I do that a smoker is his own best customer. This is how the relationship became such because I had finally fell for him in this atmosphere of degradation. But love was an infatuation that in fact had foreseen days in Oakland selling his dope and smoking my life away—suicide. There were others in prison I had watched take a shower, wake up for breakfast unable to conceal their misery and defeat at coming down from a 'hard night' and who also made their sexual frustrations known to me in hope of satisfaction. Yes; the institution of prison had been very successful in affording me a land of luxury for all the sex I could ever want. Again it was so easy to make a decision to quit the horrible addiction of crack cocaine for these wonderfully clean, sober and super fresh men. My sexuality had again been a number one element directly responsible for my continued addiction. WR was right about the untrustworthy feelings he had for me. Sex again had begun to grow cold from a very heated month or more of the nightly lust. I had begun responding with kites through the tier porters to other super-hot brothas that had been hinting that I leave WR and get with them. I became confused and frustrated very quickly. Before the end of our affair I had finally been located on the three yard. This is also where WR was prior to his going to the hole for having homemade knives "shanks" and where he met up with me after his release. He followed me less than three weeks later and a week after that we were celled up again in his cell in main population where I had hoped he would not return. As mentioned, the men on this yard were older and therefore more mature. What had happened to me including syphilis on the one yard was known by those on the three yard. They were understanding and mature about it—something one and two yards knew nothing about. But I could not execute any of the thoughts I had for any of these wonderful men because upon WR's release from the hole he claimed me as his gay boy or rather 'blade' and made me move back with him. I had to consent to him because not only were we both short I was going to Oakland when he paroled to have big time money and especially crack cocaine. My mind and sole had done nothing in the way of cleaning up to become sober once paroled let alone develop a solid plan of recovery in my life. My addiction had rested its feet firmly on the wires of my sexuality until the day I got out. In fact my addiction got mentally worse. A completely recovered physical body had harbored a more progressive mind full of addiction for almost a year behind bars. I dreamed every night and day-dreamed every day, many times a day for the day I was released and the month or so it would be for the man I now considered a trick of all tricks to parole. He even mentioned possibly being able to get a package after I got out. I had made the mistake of turning this affair into a bag of tricks with no treats. He had expressed his knowledge of my being as happy as a sissy in boy's town, but in a man's prison. He knew I was being hit on from many others for sex. But I would not go to the bathroom in the school house or other areas of the prison to satisfy those callings each day. I spent a lot of time in the library quickly becoming frustrated and disgusted trying to find out if I could actually sue the state penal system for their inadequate medical facility causing me even more seizures while in the hole before WR came along. I was approached by these innocent supper horny fellas of magnificent quality on almost a constant basis. I was looking for one brotha to cell up with or ride out on parole with—something like the day I walked on probation with that four hundred dollar check from the city jail accompanied by KV. WR's insistence of our reuniting in a cell together and picking up where we left off was confirmed. I was to parole before him and if my deviant thoughts came true I would be in the wind by the time he was out. Pressure and its frustration from the want and desire for the insistent others grew more each day. Even though there were other gays willing and eager I was with someone and knew not to mess with anyone else making me and those like me better choices over the foot loose and fancy free gays in prison. There was one incident when I was working in the law library one afternoon where I had to make a head call. I was followed by one of the more sought after fellas on the yard by gays. He did everything in his power to get me to break, but I managed to get away from his mighty and magnificent pressure. I was such a bundle of nerves until any further investigating the possibility of a law suit could no longer hold my interest that day. I remember how this and other surprise encounters like this from others turned the relationship with WR into frustration. We knew what was happening. He was no dummy. I was not in love as I thought my infatuation was back in the hole now that I was face to face with super star after super star constantly driving a secret promise of ultimate satisfaction—a hard bargain at that. There was no room in my addicted mind for planning and preparing to turn the many months with crack into reality called sobriety and its hopeful recovery. The recovery program, church and other possible help to get the process started toward a clean status and holding it which was the initial reason for coming to prison was now history. It is probably thought that I only came to prison to enjoy the multitude of men more than the willingness to achieve sobriety or better yet recovery. After WR began to rebut his notion of my having sex with others on the three yard he made life miserable for me. It ended by my refusing to go back in the cell we shared one evening after chow causing my return to the hole. I was released and put in the six house on the same three yard where I found out how much clout WR had in prison. He had his comrades attack me in the six house a couple of nights after my release from the hole. This sent me back to the hole until I was paroled only a few weeks later. But my active homosexuality was not the only reason I had deterred any thoughts of recovery in my life after prison. Epilepsy in Susie's House became an even worse problem for me during the first experience in the hole. It had frustrated me to the point of reverting back to old thoughts and behaviors centered on the old "I don't give a damn" syndrome. I remember quite well in early December, 1989 where I began experiencing problems getting the prescribed dose of seizure medication. On several occasions I was forgotten about. The first incident in December found me a period where I was not issued medication. During this period I informed both day and night nurses of their neglect. Here again is a perfect example of overcrowding and how prepared the prison system is in dealing with such a problem. This problem persisted over the approximate six months spent in this segregated unit of prison. There were numerous seizures suffered as a result. I tried to bring this matter to court and did get the initial filing done but upon release I never followed up on this suit. Guess the reason is obvious. It did however get the prison more on the ball and I did begin receiving medication as prescribed. I became so distraught during this dilemma that carried on in especially segregation until rebellion, hatred and revenge led me further into active homosexuality—I guess to stuff the pain. I may have been looking for an ease to the daily mental state I became plagued by. After the move to the side in segregation where WR was I sought relief and the company of the cellmates I had before WR moved me in his cell. Before this I had tutored four cellies having had sex a total of three nights with all other cellies until WR came along. He quickly put all thoughts of hostility and hatred on the back burner to brew until my release. The law suit was discarded from my mind after his success at completely confusing me—which was instead my own excuse seeking. He had even, at one point, took the packs my medication came in that help to prove the inconsistent sequence of my not having been issued the prescribed dose causing my grief. I had no win. I thought everyone was against me and out to get me. Sounds like paranoia on crack in the TL all over again; huh? The hierarchy of gang leaders and their members as well as prison officials were all out to see my doom. Maybe this was a message from God that I suffer like this and did not see because I came out of prison meaner and more frustrated, full of not so much revenge but eagerness to parole and find again the continued hell of crack cocaine. Up to this point there is a gay man without a family or loved ones of any kind to turn to for support. There is the thoughtless pattern of finding the right circle of friends possibly stemming from never having ventured alone to find his way in life. And there is getting caught up on the wrong page what with enticed attraction from nothing but crack addicts and life that led to this point in time. Dare say and you may admit it yourselves that I fought and lost all but the one battle so far that got me to TeeLancey Exit Recovery Program. The reason I don't include the battle to do another term in prison is because of the obvious failure from the start even though in prison I was free of active addiction. But it has been seen how the addiction is cunning in putting such active progression on hold for bigger and better outcomes that Satan reaps. I never even gave recovery and a new life a thought after the refuted efforts in trying to get involved in the school program, being a victim of negligent medical care which in my opinion was due to overcrowding, sexually and socially abused by peers (convicts in prison). All this painted a new picture for me of what prison is all about in the state of California. This is why I say there must be someone making lots of money warehousing human lives and for others there is a steady career that doesn't take much knowledge to achieve—correctional officers with opportunity from turn-key to superintendent of a prison and above. There are doctors and nurses, secretaries and other administrative staff, parole and probation officers, the court system and all the supplies and those who create, maintain and help build more prisons. Yet overcrowding was felt from jail throughout the one year spent in a system plagued by the awesome effects of new kids on the block on the corner of every hood in every city and county in our great United States addicted to crack cocaine. Compare yesterday in the 1970s and 80s when base cocaine was having its fundamental initial effects on our society in the form of crack. There seem to be a quiet period while I finished my second two year degree in prison for a second term back home. Nobody really seemed to put emphasis on heroin like crack today although it was the drug of choice up to that era. Crack was a whole new thing to me upon parole back then even though I heard it had been around for years. I do not know what made crack spring out of this era having its effect on just as many as did the Hippy era of my time with pot and acid (psychedelics) other than great social popularity. Crack is a very addictive substance being one of the peculiar psychological characteristics apart of the many highlights of the high. And I believe the mental blocking I did in prison was part of the addiction's powerful ways to put me on hold until I paroled what with all the trouble and misery I seemed to have caused myself this time in the penal system of California. But those seizures were no joke and I did not induce them purposely. Having or waking from them is no fun at all. The after effects of bitten tongue, severe headache, aching body and horrible disposition from the convulsions, spasms and other effects of epilepsy make life pretty miserable. This fact seems to be the biggest reason my addiction used to keep itself alive and well including my own stubbornness. Adding hatred to the already distraught complications of epilepsy creating fear and paranoia on a daily basis from the first day until July 24th, 1990 when I paroled, found me still addicted. On the day of parole I was given two hundred dollars which is the all too famous 'gate money', a set of clothing that kept me from looking like I indeed just escaped out of prison and a bus ride to the small town of Susanville at their bus station. From there I was on my way so to speak. I could have left for parts unknown out of state and not reported to my parole agent within the twenty-four hour deadline. After being dropped off at this site there was a sixteen dollar fee for the van transportation to Reno, Nevada's bus station. It was early afternoon by this time. I decided to walk around the biggest little city in America and check out the possible chance of copping a rock as the thoughts of using were foremost on my mind. Getting nowhere fast in this city as it was new and confusing in area to me I made it back to the bus station and boarded a 3PM bus to San Francisco. A few hours later I arrived in the city I had made a complete mess of my life in. But the thoughts of how physically clean I was after a year was suppressed by how actively addicted and still just as alive my mental and emotional addicted desires were. After arriving at the new bus depot site located further down Mission I proceeded to the very den-of-sin, the Tenderloin, and purchased two twenty-dollar rocks with some to the gate money I had left from travel expenses back to this city. I purchased the same scud missile kind of paraphernalia in the same store located on Market Street. All this was done without the thought of a place to stay or reporting to a parole agent and giving this new and important person in my life a urine test, of which were common everyday requests from them. My purpose for sobriety proved to be a fruitless effort. I had not taken all the important elements of cleaning up the nightmare of addiction to crack to heart and as well seriously. With the help of a prison system found to be an even greater battle to achieve positive success in it was easy for me to stay in the frame of mind not allowing work and readiness toward recovery to become a reality. Thus I had defeated myself again and found even deeper complications with crack cocaine after the so-called intent to recover in prison.

VI

Recycled From Prison Again
'A Cold Night in August 1990'

Addiction, homelessness, crime and the degradation that goes with
it had found me waiting in the cold San Francisco night for
morning to break whereupon I would enter the office of the
department of corrections to try and continue a solution to it all.
Suicide just isn't in my program. I want sobriety. The No Named
society is a great bunch of folks; but, I could seem to find my way
to the study of this society's total philosophy. Before being told to
"take what you need and leave the rest"; I had got caught up in my
chosen sexuality in the middle of a ball of confusion. Excuse
seeking had become a way of life. An example is my trying so hard
to enter another of many drug programs only to find no acceptance.
Some two weeks later I run into the intake counselor in the TL
purchasing his own continuous problem with life. Another example
is my spending some twelve months in prison; drug free only to
come out with a nasty attitude about the enterprise that warehouses
human lives for what seems only a business oriented entity for

114

profit. No real attempt at combating and curing the problems that lead so many lives into drugs and all its counterparts were really dealt with. There is only the bare minimum as compared to those TL hotels bare minimum that seem to please those authorities. Still another example is finding a wonderful boss to work for and finding hard labor and toil a great way to deter drugs from my mind—until that first paycheck comes along. Seems the seven days a week, sometimes 16 hours a day is a great excuse to foster the "I don't give a damn" attitude. All this and much more had finally led to the night of August 20th, 1990 where another check, of which was the first paycheck after prison, was 'poofed' away. Paranoia, fear, excuse seeking, the fight between what could be the right/left brain syndrome, loneliness, hate, lost love or simply lust and so much more were all found once again after so many months of what should have been precious clean time. It had now come to the ultimate point of 'what to do'. I tried the drug information hotline and talked to what seemed a very concerned lady who led me astray. The General Hospital's drug detox program she found after sending me out there had a three months waiting list. Nothing else could be done for those wanting an emergency exit—or a quick and easy way out to continue on with the same ole . . . She mentioned that herself. But she mentioned other places to go seek help **_TOMMORROW!!_** My current situation involving three hundred dollars' worth of crack in my system I thought must be dealt with now. My own thinking had me here in a stairwell just round the corner from the parole office on a cold Tuesday morning around three in the morning waiting for this office to open. Whatever became of this decision to again find help through such an entity will have to be seen and heard for its own worth. At least in prison with all its degradation I did find a year's worth of sobriety. Why I felt I could come out of such an entity unprepared to truly keep my life free of drugs is beyond me. I don't know if I am excuse-seeking when I express the fact that time spent in prison offered no real fortification and its therapy work needed for re-entering such a complicated society. Sure there were sobriety groups and religion of different faiths. But what about peer organizations geared toward specifically being a closer liaison for success upon parole? Rap groups, peer groups, brothas helping brothas no matter what color and such, developing support out here for those in prison, education enhancements, job training on a level geared for career obtainment once paroled and a vast pool of positive workable ideas are desperate considerations needed to make going back to a society a challenge one could actually accept and conquer. The bare minimums as it stands seem only the necessities made possible to continue the fear of success and foster an 'I don't give a damn' attitude that is only a cover-up for the fear found in achieving a positive way of life and still maintain excitement. Am I lost in a maze of pure frustration? Had I the facilities and its people to aspire to maybe I would not be sitting here now on the steps of the parole office, after being chased away from the stairwell by police, waiting on another ray of hope. Will I hear the usual from this facility how I am not trying hard enough? The difference of positive versus negative help is being paroled a lonely man with nothing but the two hundred dollars gate money eaten up somewhat by travel expenses from California's Susanville prison high in the mountains. Compare this to a group of those in society eager to help as many as possible find that chance after working so hard in a positive school program, vocational program, training in other fields, counseling on a real one-on-one level, development of a positive environment for those wanting a real chance right there inside the prison walls, social groups and basically some real honest help for those men and women who have pondered and pondered and continue to battle a new way of life—a better way found free of drugs. Why can there be a way to begin what is still going to be a hard task of achievement? Would achieving such a positive future, a clean break from degradation be worth the fight if there was something worth fighting for in such as prison? The positive atmosphere in prison I speak of would definitely be a new approach. Separating those wanting a serious break from the beginning and creating that environment for them to pay their debt to society seems like a bunch of words. To look at so many prisons harboring killer attitudes and personalities and the like along with those wanting or even just thinking about a way out together in an environment with no real help facilities seems to foster recidivism and its continuous horror found only several blocks from where I sit waiting to see what such as the department of corrections and parole will do for my own continued cry for help. To send me back to one of the more than twenty-five prison sites or a drug program depicted by the program of TeeLancey Exit Recovery Program is what I face. TeeLancey Exit Recovery Program could not find it in their hearts to work with a so-called "sexual deviant" with epilepsy. To be told that I am the one who must make it work by so many including those ex-convicts and drug users as well as those having studied criminology having never experienced the horrors one may be going through is told over and over. Not realizing or taking into consideration the fact that every human being is a very unique individual trapped in a thinking of negative basics leaves little room for aspiring or assessing a possible way out. I'm not a dumb person. Like so many of those trapped in prison without an education I have managed to put forth an effort to obtain a great start in life with the knowledge found in the school system provided by my home state's prison system. Thus I am not putting the prison system industry down completely. It is obvious the difference I see in prison systems of different states. An entire social floor for those inmates representing everything from ethnic/cultural groups to higher education can be seen and taken advantage of in the prison I achieved an education in. Not only did I work to achieve my GED but from there going on to earn two associate degrees is part of the positive help in a real environment behind bars I refer to. And what else could have been done to help overpower the demand in me with the positive asset of arts having a wonderful time progressing it only in prison during such a critical time in life? Compare this achievement to the twelve months in California's prison system where I could not even offer my graduate skills as a help on a peer level basis to those struggling to achieve their GEDs. There are gangs and racism, north versus south, Crips versus Bloods, Mexicans, Blacks, Whites adding to hatred and so much more violence. Prison, it seems, is only a place where all this ignorance can foster and grow. Fostering is a perfect depiction of prison yards with continued stabbings, murders and the like without any possible outlook for change—a change, any change, no doubt for the better. To send me back to one of these facilities would only foster a negative attitude no matter how hard I tried. My addiction as a result of twelve months in California's prison system was only put on the back burner while I dealt with my sexuality inside such a nightmare. Believe me being gay in prison is no fun if you have behaviors unlike those cross dressing and flamboyancy, flaunting and the like. Being gay in this complex society is frustrating. To come to my parole officer for help the very next day after parole due to having fallen flat on my face only to be given shelter in the very place I started this madness with crack in, again, is beyond me. Would it make sense to locate one in my situation somewhere away from the temptation and threats that cause one to makeup his or her mind to relapse? If a real chance exists for those like myself; where is it? I am aware of the power of addiction that drugs has caused in my life. Along with a continuing strong belief that I can make it; I am ready to find a communication and relationship with God in making a faithful eventual change. To do this I must seek out those actually wanting to help. Those who "have been there and done that" and want to help see me through are who I seek. If you say I can do this alone I will only be found a continuous looser and/or dead. I will only maintain the attitude so many continue to foster without hesitation day in and day out. I will only be caught up in a life of crime to support a career with drugs. Running from the truth is not what I am doing. How can I succeed without the help and love of those wanting to see a positive and serious mind, body and soul make that clean break? Can those of you after a career in this arena without the experience of an on-hands final exam or term paper proceed with the understanding many need in this kind of hard work? Forgive me if I am thinking wrong. Please show where I fail to at least try and seek the help needed to put my life on sturdy ground and most important keep it firm. Showing me, teaching me, loving me as I want so much to love seem much better than the structure outlined by an attack therapy program or the permanent degradation found in any prison yard. If I were successful in achieving sobriety on my own it would make me a real hard personality with an ugly cold heart. I could love no one but me if indeed that is called love. I'd rather be a user for the rest of whatever life I have left than to live in just as great a turmoil. Is this more excuse-seeking because I need people? Am I wrong to think this way? Am I on the right track? Are there those of you who honestly want to help? Can I continue to think positively and believe I still have hope; hope coming from those of you concerned and aware of another's dilemma in life? Are you too perfect and innocent to extend a helping hand? I continue to feel that our great United States and the world is progressing more and more toward a sorry end. Struggling to be a Higher Power here on this earth leaves little room for those wanting a way out of the traps in life on especially the lower end. Seems those in power are just too busy fighting a much bigger war of their own. Thus I among so many others must continue to suffer. Giving up would seem an easy way out. Should the day come that I have won the fight I will appreciate and cherish as well as have love in my heart flourishing more than those constantly at war around the bargaining table. Learning to hate myself will be a feeling long gone. I can't even look at the man in the mirror for I know I tell nothing by lies about my sobriety. Money, the root of all evil, makes sure I continue to loose. I continue to feel that love is stronger than money—that the power of love making is stronger than the power of money. Simply moving away from the situation is not an answer, totally. I need help. The farm at that California rehabilitation center may have been a better choice than prison or at least a better program of recovery. You can ask my last employer if indeed I do work hard. Hard work and a clean drug free environment would do more for me than the lazy degraded atmosphere found in prison or the kind of therapy found in venting so-called anger, frustration and the breaking down of the individual in an effort to rebuild a new person of which seem to foster hate. To realize and then assess the kind of help needed for an addicted individual takes a true awareness and understanding of that addicted life. There are many types of drugs which mean there are many kinds of addictions. One fact for sure is how any addiction is not an easy thing to cold turkey or just dump on your own. The will and desire, the want and need to quit can be there but still cause great amounts of problems in ending a life of such suffering. In fact most do have great difficulty. Those rare cases of straight cold turkey are to be commended. Those seemingly rare and blessed individuals should be among those who contribute their precious knowledge, experience and time keeping what they were so blessed to get for nothing and work with the great many like me having so much difficulty achieving that clean break. Help organizations such as the department of corrections, parole agencies, drug programs both in and out patient, the No Named society and the like do not seem to be truly combating the vast population of drug addiction as they may indeed would like. Compared to the numbers there are too few programs and organizations put together to make up a solid artillery force needed in this fight. More positive workable programs of all types geared for the many kinds of users and their individualities need to come into perspective. To be told there is a three months waiting list for a detox program means one who wishes or needs immediate help must, more times than not, continue to live in active addiction until space, time and the like become available. Add to this the need to be insured or able to pay a large sum of money or have the kind of money it takes to go through a treatment program designed only to detox and not truly help that addict help his or her own self come to real and actual terms with a life lived in addiction. That statement involves a lot of work, love and real understanding. Who has the insurance needed before being able to be accepted into an inpatient drug/alcohol and detox program provided the waiting list is not some weeks or months long? The wealthy and those few successful dealer/users are about the only people I can think of. When you are out there using money becomes a lost value. Crack, wine, heroin and the like keep these addicts penniless due to the huge cost of maintaining their addictions with crack being the highest priced most popular addiction during the times of these writings. Alcohol of course is lower priced but it is a legal substance making it just as dangerous. It is believed that other adductions are not as intense as the crack addict; who will spend every dollar on crack until the money is completely exhausted. They can wait out whatever continuous period before money is once again obtained; i.e.: paycheck (daily, weekly, bi-monthly, monthly), GA checks including Food Stamps, SSI checks, street hustle including robbery, burglary, panhandling, prostitution and the like. When this money comes, on whatever kind of schedule it has, the entire amount is consumed within a matter of minutes, hours or if lucky a few days. Never will such last and be spaced and distributed throughout each pay period as if one held a respectable job with a long time bank account. This is the 'tweek' and 'geek' process known throughout. I have no idea how or why this psychological pattern makes one act in such very strange ways mentally, but as expressed it is known how this craving process can keep the crack addict continually spending until all funds are again depleted. Sex in most cases play an important role where it is used to keep the sex object interested and the buyer attracted. Many times sex will be unsuccessful because paranoia will set in usually on the buyer's end but both can initiate this mental condition. This will cause any sum of money to drain with visit after visit to the dealer until exhausted. I don't know what other chemicals and such are added to make the hard cocaine substance called crack but through experience I am very familiar with the out-of-the-norm deviant mental behavior pattern it has from continued smoking. I do know that in order to try or think you are relieving this psychological behavior takes these continued return trips to the 'dealer/doctor'. The preceding documentation expressed the addiction to crack I suffered from its beginning to its climax. After throwing away a year's worth of sobriety achieved in prison came the full gut of remorse, self-pity, anger and most of all for me the fear. Getting on my feet with a place to stay and food to eat was always achieved after a run. This time I had found employment. A job as a janitor cleaning movie theatres had afforded me the luxury of gaining some sense of pride. This did not take a more definite effect until a cold night experienced in August—even though I suffered with this addiction more from this point on. Having found myself still ignorant to true sobriety and getting high only minutes after parole back into the city I got the job as janitor, a place to stay in the TL of course and a few clothes as well as food. But the trick for me was keeping those thoughts of "one won't hurt" from totally doing what I allowed myself to do at the site of a three hundred dollar paycheck earned for a week on this or any job for that matter. I began to think that if I earned or cleared this amount in just one week I would be able to afford to get high and keep a place to stay and other essentials. Excuse seeking and finding those ways and means to keep using found me buying just one more hit which turned into the nightmare suffered August 20th. No room was allowed in my thoughts for the security of a roof, food and transportation to work to earn another paycheck so that I could do it all over again—the psychological effects of the blast! So I ended up broke, homeless, tweeked and geeked out, scared, confused and who knows what else. Like the first day I got out of prison and got loaded, I went to my parole officer to turn myself in. Again I was not violated. I was not breaking the law so much. I was a sick man in a disease where I had not taken that first step totally to heart. And before I could begin to realistically and honestly attempt recovery and succeed I had to do this. This I did not find out even after that "cold night". I was helped out again by my parole officer. My job was not trashed as a result of this run on crack in the three short weeks out of prison. I was given another chance—another of so many up to this point since being an addict progressively getting worse. No, my friend, I kept right on planning and thinking I was tough enough to take the chances enabling me to continue using. So I went through a drug program prescribed by my parole officer (PO). It was an outpatient program which meant I came to the parole office twice a week for urine analysis testing (UA). I decided it would be in my favor if I quit for the four months that I would be in this program. In this time I could get myself back together and stay sturdy on my feet. I was instead planning a horrible run and its inevitable consequences. If I go through these urine tests clean I would get off parole and be able to save money, get a place and most of all purchase a big enough 'sack' to begin something I was never any good at doing—selling dope! Working this plan found my job restored, a nice enough place to stay located in the TL, food to eat, a savings account and what looked like a positive future. I went to my boss and poured my addicted heart out to him. We became friends and I asked him to be my guardian (mentor). We opened up an account together and he put the next few checks I earned in this account. Whenever I needed to do things positive with my money he was there. This is how I got the studio apartment in the TL, bought food, clothes and lived without crack enabling me to maintain a clean urine test each time for the entire four month outpatient program. When thoughts came about of wanting to use due to stimulations for mainly sex I thought about the end result of my waiting—not of the actual consequences of using. Even though this worked I grew weary because of planning to continue using after this program had been a foremost on my mind causing my wanting even more to use with each passing day. I was able to do a year in prison here in California free of drugs. Back home I was drug free for years at a time in prison. Thus I thought it was no big deal to plan continued active addiction and be able to do it better. This was actually how I shunned the desire to use each day that passed during this time. What the hell happened to the desire to quit for good? Thoughts of the day I could buy a big bag and grab a sex object of which were plentiful in the TL kept me strong or should I say kept my addiction strong using this kind of thought pattern. Even though I continued to grow weary of waiting for that day to come I managed to wait through what turned out to be an entire six month program. I was able to achieve two theatre accounts and work them seven days a week. Many days were spent putting twelve hours cleaning and maintaining these accounts allowing time to grow closer more rapidly. I did not use and remained true to the original plan. There were many thoughts of actually quitting. Counter thoughts of that first hit after all the time spent cleaning up and the sex that would come with it overpowered any thinking about getting a real life or going out and using right now as I had the money to do so—the powerful effects of relapse are so awesome and cunning! Spending all this time working so hard for what I believed so intensely to be my reward for doing a great job found me going to required No Named meetings in the bay view area and putting on a phony face for those folks and those authorities at the parole department. School began infiltrating my thoughts after sometime because I have this desire to finish up my BA. And in October of that year I began inquiring and preparing for San Francisco's state university. This is the part of me I speak of defining it as the right/left brain theory where my good thoughts and its artillery (wanting to complete school) battled with the negative part of my thinking being my addiction. Working kept me making over a thousand dollars a month during this drug program. When my boss needed help at other theatres I was there for him. His being my boss and guardian kept money at my disposal and kept it stacking up in my savings account as well. I refused myself positive things in order to continue this planned relapse. When I was finally close to the successful completion of the drug program I had accumulated over six hundred dollars in the bank free and clear. Rent was paid up for six weeks and there were no other bills to worry about. I was graduated about a month before the four months because of the phony face and clean testing that proved to them my having become a changed man. Planning for entrance into the university cinched my early graduation—more cunning and underhanded maneuvering by the addict in me. And it was that I wasted no time getting this reward party under way for my addiction the very day I was given my certification of completion. Here is that lie: The fear of survival, life, freedom, AIDS and other diseases and the paranoiac list goes on was upon me now after parole once again. In my condition upon entering your doors August 20th, 1990 after another no-win situation or better yet bout with crack cocaine I had made up mind to do something and do something positive and real this time. My addiction was more than I could deal with any longer. Coming out of prison after twelve months sober only to find the first paycheck after prison blown completely sky high full of crack was just not something that could continue. I truly believe my parole agent could see a true desire to become free of the chains of continued use and find a turnaround in my favor. He could see I had some fight left and had not given up to the all too famous "I don't give a damn" attitude. Thus my name mysteriously came out the hopper for the CARD program. I have no regret of being placed in this program for some three months. I found the positive interaction at the bay view area center a real treat. Those of my own background made it so easy for me to be able to relate and become comfortable in an effort to open up and put sobriety in perspective. All those sobriety groups were a treat I still want to attend. Testing became a ritual of sorts because of the continued finding of no drugs and alcohol that continued to become a stronger and more courageous battle I am fighting to win. I mean, each day becomes easier to face as time becomes part of my asset instead of the detriment time had been for me so much in the past. Add to this the realization of my 39 years—no spring chicken. My past had seen some good things. My education to date would be a real challenge today to complete with the accomplishment so far of two associates and GED. This would seem like putting a loose or missing screw in a fine piece of machinery—the only missing link needed for a successful life. We shall see. Thanks to this program I have had the help in staying powerful and strong whether I knew it or not. Time in this program with clean time to think on a daily basis had lifted my spirits to an all-time high. I am aware of how I must take it a day at a time and do it very easy. These are some tools to use now at this stage of such a wonderful feeling. By the same token I must admit feeling only cautiously great! So great is my determination and feeling until I am now into my third day cigarette free. A crutch was all I needed to get me started and I found it on 'National Smoke-Out Day' which I found the day I turned my application package in for hopeful admittance to San Francisco State University. Values and morals are becoming a very important part of my life which is something I really never gave much credit to prior to a career in prison and very seldom gave much thought to during the heat of addiction. I thank the CARD program in the bay view area for the outstanding overseers helping me see and stay on this positive fantastic road I know I have finally accomplished once and for all!

Thanks CARD, all those of the department of parole, the No Named society and all the positive faces and situations I've been able to learn from and aspire to. As well thanks for letting me live in the Tenderloin without the desire to involve myself in the use of drugs and instead practice my ever reminding ways to just say; "Hell No"! To see and be freshly stimulated by the day in and out sadness of all that crack can and will do is another tool I've put to use as part of my recovery. AIDs and the rest of life's diseases in this world are here to remind me of what I could be facing at this very moment had I not chosen the desire to be free of such a life and as well actually feel the seriousness of such a true actuality. Those out there who must take that first step and admit to such a problem are scared away every time by the ease of another 'hit' compared to actuality. I mean; it really takes a lot to find help after becoming aware of one's own addiction—it ain't easy. Places like this detox and emergency outlet are not taken seriously enough. Money is needed to put a real force together to help those who run into the difficulty that can deter them instead of help them along on the right road to recovery. I remember the many times I ran into walls that could very well have kept up my using today. Some are not as strong as I may have been. Some or others need a push. The want is there, the desire great; but, lost again for many needing detox hung out to dry on a three month and more waiting list, insurability before acceptance into a program, narrow prejudice minded ideologies found in other so called help organizations from Hot-line programs and the like. If you will look at my record you can see that I was begging to keep from becoming a lost cause. I know I have lots of fight. I am being rewarded for sticking it out and finding that vehicle I need to help me reach the sight of the all too famous road to recovery—the mountain top. I may be adding too much here but I do indeed feel great. And that vehicle I found after so much bull-shit was the CARD program. Confidence is part of my everyday morning wakeup now—not the high. Making it through another day with a four point GPA and having added another important element of time to the never ending and ever growing vast majority of time I have now has me feeling this good today. Tomorrow looks only too great and yesterday is a tool I use to continue learning from. Again, in closing, thanks CARD and all the other good people, places and things of today. Please do me one favor for those suffering like I did only a few months ago and allow for an easier channel to make that desire a reality by knocking down that impossible brick wall. Many of us have this weakness to alcohol and drugs. Being the unique individuals we are we cannot do a basic one, two, three of recovery . . .

Boy! If you only knew the hell I went through. My addiction was frightened of my parole officer. As well it was cautious of him and used its cunning and baffling skills to the fullest command in getting the parole department off my back so that I would be free to use. My addiction was successful in doing this. This led to party after paycheck. Every single paycheck was consumed in crack except for paying the rent which I had become accustom to paying during those ninety days of only abstinence. I was successful with the plan over this period of time. If the letter to the department of parole can be seen for the moral value I believe it has there can be detected the cry to clean up coming through this cunning cover-up a part of my addiction's arsenal. But this had always been there in the end when I sought relief from the many bottoms and brick walls I constantly ran into. Only when I hit these bottoms would I come clean and ask for help or begin to sing the song of "help". I guess this happens to those addicts who do in fact let true feelings out when it may seem too late. The three months plus plan of relapse, if it is called such, was the ultimate show of my addiction to crack. And I did in fact carry on with my addiction for over two months after the ninety day program before I hit bottom once again. This run was the nightmare that saw even bigger paychecks than those prior runs the year before. Remember the statement I elaborated on about people and our individualities? That even though we have those basics we still are very different in thought and actions. There is always that one very familiar to us all that tries to contradict what I expressed about our unique differences. It is a great escape and denial of whatever problem one might face such as my addiction. It simply states that we are all the same and therefore bound to making the same mistakes. I will go for the second part of this common belief or expression among us but not the first. I made it perfectly clear that we were all very unique individuals among a set of basics. We all have ten fingers, two arms, two legs, a heart, two eyes, a mind and basically we all have the same makeup. But with these basics do we all think exactly alike, look alike (maybe identical twins), love alike, feel alike and generally live alike? I've also heard somewhere down the line that if such were the case and we were all exactly or even similar under the basics of life how this would be a pretty boring and dull place to only exist in. Add to this the confusion of trying to differentiate each other constantly leaving no room for pleasures in life but only the pain and turmoil of this constant boring confusion. This repeated cycle, better termed as insanity, may contribute to the effects of addiction. Finding a new high each time I chose to spend another paycheck kept me constantly searching for the time I had experienced the ecstasy I thought it was the first time so long ago. Remembering Reggie and how I felt for the very first time in my life left me with a journey I suffered from that point on. From this point on after the so called successful completion of the CARD program saw more of the very same. It saw continued checks murdered by my addiction without any reservation of the only outcome that happened every time I was paid. An example of continued insanity was reuniting old so-called friendships that vanished into thin air each time money depleted with the insane spending on crack. One of the most heartbreaking affairs came

129

back into my life after the total run in the Tenderloin, TeeLancey Exit Recovery Program and prison all covering almost three years. This also included the CARD program lasting almost four months. There were new affairs I kept repeating during this time that were no different in results than that of EJ. My weakness for EJ is not something I can express well. As mentioned he involved more of the affair this second time around leading me into continued and progressive using. I had to have more crack in order to experience the ultimate sexual experience EJ and I had. I knew he was a man who would have sex with another man as long as his role was completely masculine or dominate. I had no idea he was just as bisexual as I. I never knew he would one day ask me to do to him what I had enjoyed from him so many times in our past. I also did things of a homosexual nature I never thought I would or could ever do. But the insanity of the high continued to find new ways and means of bringing back that 'oh so wonderful, ultimate and original feeling' of lust that seemed at this new time so very long ago. To know I am not alone in these thoughts of achieving that one specific time during initial smoking, shooting or drinking patterns was confirmed by what EJ and I shared this second time around. But the sex was never complete because of the paranoia we both faced due to his coming out of such a closet door and my becoming so overwhelmed by a more enhanced sexual relationship. I have never really had such an enhanced sexual encounter with a gay partner which made the experience of "flip/flopping" a tool used to keep the crack the front runner. It was either or. Keeping the drama of the sex at a low level will not let me divulge the sex incident itself. From what I have expressed about the insanity of the high we both were infected by is more than enough to create in the mind the exact picture of our looking for a better way to enjoy a high that had long since been destroyed by time and its addiction to crack. To elaborate more on the insanity itself found me achieving other sex in search for any satisfaction I could not get from my disease. Think about it for just a minute. Wonder if any sexual denomination be it: homosexual, heterosexual, bi-sexual and those super freaks that appear on the news for their sexual desires gone haywire; that are led by the power of addiction? EJ had begun to loose consistency and I again began to feel the pressure my money was having on this relationship. I had the feeling his show of freedom from the 'closet' was a way for him to put a seal on our addicted relationship. Instead I sought out other affairs. One unique affair was a very dark, very good looking, very southern black ex-boxer from Mississippi who I could swear to this day had made me fall in love. I worked my job as a janitor very hard to achieve paydays where we smoked everything except the rent needed to keep him sheltered there with me for as long as I could. I forgave him for running off with money I gave him to cop for us. I forgave him for stealing from me, for lying and being the average Tenderloin crack addict whore/toss-up with exceptional looks and features he knew could only make him a prostitute in such as the TL. Keep in mind my expressed views about how men make far better prostitutes than women. Women can seldom lay up for days at a time like men can and simply vanish into thin air, be accepted and forgiven and craved over and over by the same victims. It is my belief through my own experience as a prostitute or better termed toss-up that women cannot do this better than men. Many women out there have children and are not as strong to weather the storm of spreading oneself around with such consistency. A flat fee; "vip, vam, thank ya mam" and that's all 'she' wrote. It's time to move on cause' I got kids to take care of". Not only is there my opinion, there are those comments and opinions I get from other gays and women that make my evaluation of men a pretty sound one. And in recovery houses and such are found more men who suffer the ramifications of addiction than women or others which can also lead me to believe how man is in fact the dominate party involved with addiction and the means and ways of maintaining such a 'jones'. But I do not take women for granted or at all too lightly as the addiction is a very devious and cunning infection in any human being's life. In recovery I also heard something that struck me as very true. If you have noticed there is one organization I have not talked much about—good or bad. This is because I love this society and the people in it. They have made more sincere sense out of the term recovery and the real meaning of sobriety than I have ever heard and endured in any program, prison, religion or other entity of help. Their philosophy and the way it works has meaning and substance one can put to work in achieving real suggestions, possibilities and coming up with one's "own" actual answer—one's own real 100 percent decision. Once one gets a head full of their philosophy using can become the vehicle on that road to hitting a bottom needed many more times than not to make the decision expressed among "peers". Having been introduced on my own to this group of wonderful folks long before the time and date of these writings found me the victim of punishment. All the paranoid feelings and especially the guilt trips I continually found were part of having this head full of something that stuck in my mind. I believe this entity is largely responsible for all the crazy things I did and the decisions made during all the wild continuing of an addiction that I knew had to come to an end one way or another—bottom. The CARD program, TeeLancey Exit Recovery Program and how I got there; prison, the self-help center, that farm I wanted and one guilty trip after another continued to fail. My knowing or able to pick up on a message that was definitely being relayed was absent through it all. And there was a lot I went through. Only some of its intensity has been presented here. Addiction is generally a multitude of years of which I suffered through a total of more than three decades. Before the end of the nightmare after prison and CARD there were experiences and all its drama that led me to the beginning of seeing the messages and paying attention to them, heeding at least some of the advice, the advice found within myself sparked what my own worst enemy fought so hard to keep me from seeing. Friends I thought I made turned out to be a lesson through experience that will let me learn and grow in the positive direction I had only thought about but never gone full force with. Addiction after the high had become the habit which does not allow clarity in thought for any length of time. Thinking about recovery with a head full of a particular recovery program cannot be evaded, commonly resulting from the nightmare of insanity: "There must be a better way. How can I achieve such? Where do I look? Who do or can I turn to?" But through no avail life continues past these thoughts and continues on with the insanity. Another paycheck comes along, tax returns that put too much money in one's pocket, selling or trying to sell drugs that only made me, the salesman my own best customer, GA and Food Stamps that turn into a bi-monthly run month after month and the disease goes on and on. Desperation time after time only finds temporary solutions and relief due to not being able to stuff the pain of addiction with "just-one-moe". Surrendering completely to this nightmare will not happen for many until that endless amount has become more than the addict can handle. So I smoked and I continued to smoke thinking after the CARD program I had done the ultimate in getting to a point where I could feel comfortable smoking crack without urinalysis tests and constant worry of parole agents and the like on my back. All during the six months after prison I managed to keep the janitorial job that kept me working from paycheck to paycheck. Life meant nothing more or nothing less to me than the satisfaction of another bag of crack, kibbles, bits, pebbles and crumbs depending on whatever and however funds became available. Why I thought I could register for college and complete my education at least to a bachelors was easily seen the day I received the grant money I combined with a paycheck from work to go on another wild tough pattern leading me again to think "this time I will achieve those different, better, more exciting and more satisfying results". The end result was again and was always the very same insane thinking with its very same insane results. Expecting different results after so many, many times began to pile skyscraper high. Add to this the wonderful entity I mentioned that I had gotten a head full of interrupting the finding of any comfort getting high and achieving pleasure—yah; especially sex. I can look back through the experiences and traumas prior to release from prison and see a pattern of living that had changed dramatically. No longer was I not paying rent in order to maintain a place to get high. No longer did I move from place to place due to hotline and GA hotels in order to retain the entire welfare check used strictly and entirely for crack. No longer could I not at least try to keep something to eat provided I could get it before purchasing crack. No longer did I question buying at least some of the comforts of home including personal hygiene. All these things of life and more were considered greatly after coming out of prison twelve months free of only the physical damages of addiction before going through another bout with drugs—again the unconscious planning of another relapse. And the disease as a result of those twelve months in a prison atmosphere may have made it much easier to simply progress and plan such an ending as it can in such an environment. Not having sought out any positive support and help to combat and deal specifically with addiction while in prison and the CARD program allowed the cunning powers of addiction to escalate. Here is where being ready to allow sobriety another of so many tries to actually come in and do the job needed to win the battle over addiction was lost again letting me feel the outcome of relapse being such a powerful force inside me. War and relapse at this point have the same meaning. Sobriety having a set of troupes that do indeed thwart the evils of addiction allow serenity a chance to be experienced where total serenity can come into focus as this war continues to be fought—footwork. Getting to this stage of experiencing serenity means giving it not just a try but surrendering one's entire self to winning this war. Until that could happen life continued to be what it was for me—a losing battle. Paychecks kept their dates with dealers, as did the gafflers who burned and the sex objects that meant nothing anymore. I was only going through the motions without a conscious awareness of where my life was at. People were always willing to make new friends and try to develop sexual relationships with me due to word getting 'round like it does in the 'hood'. There was even a so called friend whose brotha simply smoked the entire sack of crack I gave him to sell for me. I should have seen or comprehended the strong message I was given when he was found hours later in the film den (porno shop) with an excuse of having been arrested with all the money. But I continued on and on. The old "I don't give a damn" attitude kicked right into high gear and saw more and more insanity. It led to the achievement of a grant and registration for those classes at SFSU that I never pursued. It was even found that I would begin at junior status instead of a sophomore or any beginning point in a university due to my work in community colleges. In other words another message had again been planted right before my eyes for me to take advantage of an opportunity to escape instead of planning what was more relapsing. All the guilt trips, messages, bad experiences and denial that continually built up finally led me to again make another try at doing something about it. It is so strange though how I one day decided to put an end to it all and give myself that break heard about through this entity I did not know I had a head full of. I first quit the job I had without any reservations of what I was going to do afterwards—I just quit. All I thought about was getting the last check, smoking it up, checking out of the apartment I had and committing myself to anyplace where I could simply clean up—*AGAIN!* Doing it this way would lead one to think I only wanted to clean up so that I could start over fresh with a new job, new settings and such in a new chapter in this continued story of addiction. Instead I smoked this last check up and found again the dismay of satisfying my sexual distorted desires. I checked out of the apartment leaving the manager a note asking him to pray for me because of an addiction I was now beginning to face head on. From here I went to a church in the city where I had corresponded with one of the pastors previously during this dilemma of drug use. He was not there upon arriving and I ask if I could wait for him. The affirmative reply found me moments later on my knees in the church letting a siege of repentance out to our Higher Power. This lasted for what seemed over an hour and I was escorted to the prayer room to finish out all the admitting of being so weak and prolonged without a care in an addiction that had plagued me mentally, emotionally, spiritually and physically for three years in this new and strange city of San Francisco. After all the tears and the long conversation with our Higher Power I felt a sense of humbleness and its ease. A good feeling was with me and strength enough to pack a small back pack of essentials and important papers left from the wreckage just experienced and leave the Tenderloin. I was given a bible and a book called From Prison to Praise which I read at a fast food place just around the corner from where I had experienced so much of the turmoil of crack cocaine. This message was very encouraging for me as it talked of true experiences of miracles and such that our Higher Power will put in one's life if that individual allows surrender to become that winning factor in such a war—putting it in His hands. Healing and problem solving occurred because the people in this book chose to ask Him for the help and chose to find Him. There were stories in this reading that saw tears in my eyes. I read this paperback from cover to cover in that all night eatery that last very early morning spent smoking crack in the TL or anywhere in San Francisco. Why I can recall this date, February 21, 1991, is beyond me to this day. The courage and strength I possessed afterwards found me at the last emergency shelter ever experienced in San Francisco while I waited for that next business day to arrive so that I could do what I had been in the process of doing to get out of the ugly problem faced by any individual addicted to drugs.

Make A Change BeBop

Life, my life today, is the beginning of great meaning.

Yesterday is the ending of an evil within still pending.

As I grow stronger in this new world of mending;
there is found this evil within descending.

Although this evil continues its kindling;
I forge ahead with positive rendering;
overpowering yesterday's venting.

Today there is indeed new growth.
From this day on I take on my most important oath.

No longer will I continue to coat; a life I've
lived today only to stay afloat.

My recovery is not a scape goat;
I seem to have let myself all these years tote.

There is more of me I want, desire and need to devote.
There is more of me to love and take note; now that I am woke.
The experiences at hand are all part of
the plan; to help me understand;
I am still yet a successful human.

I ask your continued help God.
Will you acknowledge with Your famous kind nod?

VII

Cry Me a Real River
September 19ᵗʰ, 1992

Another inpatient rehabilitation center saw its completion at the donation center's ARC. Was I again a success? Was I again "cured"? Could I now become a real part of life and be that success in life after such a bout with addiction? Again I was only in remission. I was only in the planning stages of another run. I had only set myself up again for failure. But this time I did not consciously plan the setbacks that came after the donation center Adult rehab program's successful completion. Guess you know by now that anyone can successfully complete a rehab program. I wanted out of San Francisco and yearned for my home in Seattle. Even though I saw the good side of this big city by the bay I was frightened of its size and therefore overpowering effects on life and the addiction I still continued to fight. Hard work in the ARC's rehab program lasted six months. This time without any straight out planning but instead the thoughts of starting over back home. And it was I graduated from this program and was given clearance by California parole authorities to go back home after success at the ARC. I did not continue to use at this point. It seemed I had come to an end of active addiction after six months of no active using, hard word, program meetings and its therapy geared toward helping one help his or her self and other factors making up the abstinence from using for the amount of time it lasted. And on mama's birthday, August 22nd, 1991, I graduated from the ARC on the bay in San Francisco. From there it was indeed a trip home to find mother had been violently taken by heart problems suffered by problems of addiction. How many of us are there who suffer alcoholic, drug addicted parenting? Mother had become a 'potna' in crime with the same evil addicted force hunting us. Other family members were involved as well. My sister got out pretty early with the birth of my nephew. She was only fourteen years old when Dell came into our lives. He was raised by mother as well after her achieving custody rights because, I guess, of my sister's adolescent age. On I went to find out that my only aunt had also past due to lung cancer. Why this was no shock to me as well as mother's death came from watching my aunt chain smoke the many Benson and Hedges cigarettes. I remember how she would light up another cigarette before putting out the last one or letting the last cigarette burn out and lighting another one within minutes. The smell of such a smoking disease did not stop me from experiencing this habit as well—along with my brotha and cousin. Then there was a second of three uncles who also past of heart failure. Heart disease is part of my family history causing my own symptoms of a heart murmur and high blood pressure. All the family negativity led to its breakup. Even though I tried to get in contact with the few family members left I had no real luck in doing so. Hate, I found, had overpowered any love there definitely was in my family. I continue to love mother even though my only brotha and sister had achieved bad feelings for her. Seems I should be the one with all the bad feelings as I was the one 'blackballed' out of the three of us. I still believe she was a wonderfully domestic woman with artistic value in the home. And I believe this is how I was given the gift of visual focus with my pastels. To see what mother did to some old drapes bought for little money at one of our favorite shopping stores would take one's breath away. She could even restore and lay carpet bought second hand from the donation center. By the time she dressed the windows in their new attire after her own make-over with dying, pleating, sewing, even dying and laying carpet, doing the same with bed spreads, furniture and the entire house; one would think it was all brand new. She was a wonderful cook as well. I know my brotha and sister will never forget the many Christmas Gumbo dinners that replaced the traditional turkey each year. And she worked super hard to get her kids that she loved presents. I'll never forget and I know Arthur can't forget the pair of full size Firestone two wheelers we got for Christmas back in the mid-1960s. Then came a dear cousin's experience of another death after my auntie with one of her own daughters losing her life very early in her teenage years. This seemed to be the finale and extent of my family that seem to tear us a part. Mother, my auntie and uncles were very hard working survivors with success, not just struggling people. They were fighters for life even though alcohol and some drugs had infiltrated their lives and into their off spring's future—us. So what was I to do now that I was back in Seattle with all the news of family having finally broken up mainly due to death? Such was a perfect reason for the evils of Satan's right hand man, addiction, to seek relief of my confused and hurt thoughts and emotions. A hit would and indeed found its way to the draw strings that closed the window of reality not having to deal with what it was I was up against. I was alone, frightened even more than I had ever been in life, confused about where and what to do from this point on here in Seattle with no family to seek emotional comfort and love and in need of immediate help. From the time I came back to Seattle, the second half of 1991, I became the same victim of addiction and its hitting another of so many bottoms finding me in shelters and mission all over again—this time at home in Seattle. Hey; such a life can be found in any city in America and probably the world. I continued to hide from the reality of life. I knew for some reason it was just too much for me to bare. I remember though how I began to seek something. I began to resist the ugly familiar feelings of addiction that had become a part of my life for another of so many times—this time here at home with no family to aspire to. I remember writing down and keeping with me some of these beginning thoughts: It's July 29, 1992 and I am still an addict. Maybe it would seem, after over six months clean and sober in San Francisco, that sobriety may have been successful and the ongoing process of recovery a part of my life. And in many ways this is true. I continue to this day to fight denial many times before a paycheck, now earned back home in Seattle, is murdered. And here at home I find the difference of a huge city compared to a big city. Unknown to me death brought me back to Seattle. Multi deaths in my family included my mother, a second of three uncles and my only aunt. Need I remind myself that all three deaths occurred within a few years of each other and most important, while I was in San Francisco geeked out (late 1980s to 1991)? Cleaning up my act so I could face this reality may be in many minds that know my situation of addiction and now the tragedy suffered in my family. It is still not known why I chose to fight back the power of this monster in me before finding out the sad news here at home. Being tired of the run down condition that began to take over was only another excuse. So many others in their addiction go far beyond the few years I spent in San Francisco tweeked out on crack cocaine. What happened after hearing the sad news about my family that caused the decision to come back home? Having been paroled from Susanville's penal institution on July 24th, 1990 and spending more months of hell with more crack cocaine I found the ARC operated by the Donation center in San

Francisco. That is when I gathered a record six months sobriety time actually looking and leaning toward recovery. Upon graduation I thought moving and living on my own was part of the reward for having become completely healed from the forces of addiction. Even though using was in my frequent thought pattern and as well frequent dreams I did not use. I believe I was honestly trying to thwart the monster within. But this form of being or existing is still known as planning to go back out—relapsing. In other words no matter the time achieved clean I was still planning to go back out whether or not I thought I was healed. Did I try to fight off the thoughts of continued use and overpower such a force? Can't really say at this point. And in fact these thoughts and dreams came to light upon achievement of my residence at what was supposed to be a clean and sober apartment complex located in the midst of San Francisco's TL . . . And on mom's birthday August 22nd, 1992: No! I have done it again! I never quit. Over and over I hear those famous words in the No Named program; "to achieve sobriety and get honestly involved in recovery one has to want to quit". All those days to date spent in pity the day after another nightmare on Crack Street do not fit these famous words. I am continuously defeated by another episode of addiction plaguing me and my sexual desires. The kind of life I am constantly attracted to will never allow me to find the desire needed so much and so badly. At 41 years old I am still a gay man whose sexual preference lies in the jocks of my own black male culture who are plagued by addiction as well. And those of us addicted to life in this lane are not at all an entity to feel comfort, love and progress amid. Add this progressive madness with the years and one will indeed find a decaying brothahood of people. Why I come to this summation comes from obvious statistics. My memory is not the best by far but I do remember for a good starting point my first impression of prison upon entering Monroe's Reformatory here at home in 1972. The reason I remember this so well is due to my sexuality. Keep in mind my preference in man. Never had I been so welcomed by my own culture. I had ideas that prison would not be so dominated by my brothas; but there they all were. Having done a lot of jail time in Seattle did not change my mind. Jail in Seattle and San Francisco were indeed dominated by Blacks. This silly notion I held was a result of my thinking that San Francisco and Seattle were big cities and its status held many other territories that were predominately White. Thus that would even everybody out behind bars. Well; Blacks held the title for being the largest population better known as the majority not minority behind these bars. I learned very quickly the needs, desires and well-being of my brothas in this setting. In Monroe I found my own open door to things hidden within me during a dysfunctional rearing as a child. Not only did I find the talent for art but went directly on to discover academics. This achieved me my GED and two associate degrees before the final days of Monroe—two terms served. Having learned how to braid my brotha's hair was also was not only a plus for me but I became very good at it. Corn-row and French design soon found me the most sought after stylist in prison. Other areas in my life opened up a world of self-esteem and its counterparts. I specifically remember the constant 3.2 grade point average (GPA) level of achievement during seven years of school which, after almost two years spent earning my GED, were college courses. My art flourished as well having become a portrait artist in my medium. All this as a result opened up a closet door I hid in for so many years. My Black brothas were very attracted to me not only because of all the new and fresh talents but more important many times for most of them was my ability to ease the pain of doing 'hard time'. Who else in prison can take the place of his wife or long time girl and his Romeo playin' women in prison other than those of my sexual gender? Many of my brothas went as far as to actually fall in love or rather become infatuated by the symbols of home we became to them. What amused me is how the administration and

143

its staff looked at such affairs and its activity as a mental illness more than sexually frustrated. Another way to see the hardship of such frustration are the many times I caught, purely by accident in open view of the showers during broad day, those masturbating without the worry or care of being caught. And there were times I helped a brotha out. Much can be expressed about prison and its everlasting effects found on the streets of what is supposed to be termed a free society. Instead it is again seen how the patterns developed in prison paved the way for today's crack hotels and residences, the foundations being spoiled by the takeover of homelessness, addiction and the like, the parks now full of alcoholism and addiction (now of all cultures mixed together) and neighborhoods now full of gangs and violence whose only mission is to destroy their own culture. Man! Does this make any sense to you? And under the guise of "our free society" there is only so much one can do to provide a way to eliminate this self-destructing time bomb. At this point I am a damn snitch—right? But who am I snitching on—my own culture or those in control who have indeed shared in the destruction of not only the majority in such grief and pain but as well a healthy chunk of all other peoples living in this free society? And please do not try to contradict with how other parts of this world we live in are worse off. Seems we have a taste of everything plaguing our world right here in the United States of America we call our 'Backyard' what with addiction, AIDS and other even more recent diseases constantly becoming a major known setback in our lives—another fact dominated by my own culture. Wonder if, by this time, one can begin to see why I believe my own culture is a prime target of their own destruction made easy by, again, this guise of a free nation. Is there any real kind of wisdom coming out of another proven statistic—the one to ten out of every one hundred or more individuals who do indeed hold long and even lifetime recovery records? Instead of just listening to war stories and "if I can you can" philosophies may be there could be included something one can hear that may indeed help bring a progressively endangered world more in focus about its problems—one being addiction. Sure we make it known by classing all our problems: diseases of all kinds, poverty, crime, violence, homelessness and the like. But are not all these problems of a secondary nature the result of the same human lives causing and fighting a major problem among us—war? To take another human life (murder) and only be punished for it by six years of prison time is another example of the real problem. This human life will then become a part of a system that will institutionalize him or her. Because of the sexual stigma attached to my Black culture, especially male, he will many times experience someone like me or even seek me out. The iron pile (weightlifting yard) will not only attract him but as well many times get him truly initiated into today's gangbanging violence. Even if one does his level best to rise above any of the lower level life styles so use to all of one's life there is found an ever tougher battle than maybe realized after a long six to eight year average normal prison term: achievement of a GED, higher education likely but rare and probably the achievement of the hardest is the look at one's self. In an environment like prison one may choose to accept the problems life had brought him or her and continue on under the acceptance of those entities inside prison enhancing or escalating those same problems into gang, institutionalization, hatred, prejudices, revenge and the like. There are others who do indeed go on to change an unwanted life of the past for a positive one. Others may indeed get caught up in what may be termed the 'mix' where even if he or she has taken advantage of the positive channels for upgrading, refining by educating and finding a new spiritual foundation of a positive nature there can still be found a lost battle at thwarting old ideas, long held relationships, customs and rearing's. Such a 'mix' can indeed be frustrating—ask me—I know. Thus even with an education afforded in prison which can be rewarding in achievement, new found talents and a sense of wanting something positive there can be the biggest battle in making that true transition to a positive source. The No Named fellowship is certainly right about denial and excuse seeking. It is a popular tool used by the monster in an addict to justify another hit of crack, shot of heroin, drink of alcohol or whatever. An example is my own problem having been caught in the mix under my own circumstances. Crack has no tender feeling. Addiction is indeed a powerful, cunning and baffling entity. It does indeed care less about death; only the achievement of that next hit. It can lay patiently knowing its plans for that next run is indeed being executed during the course between paydays, welfare checks, food stamps, robberies, burglaries or by whatever means necessary. And where will it all end? I've experienced everything except my own death, even though near death is certainly included. And when one has two addictions working together who share common interests life can be pretty rough regardless of an interesting and fulfilling education achieved in prison, an art talent or whatever else positive. To combine the positive artillery to combat a drug and sex addiction can help during those 'days after'. Maybe one can get further between times of using enough to assess the true desire to quit. Being given advice by different people concerning my frustrated life has caused me to become an even more skilled damn liar in an effort to keep my sexual desires alive and well satisfied. The latest gift, talent or whatever it may be termed for writing has afforded me a way to communicate all the ills plaguing me without all the embarrassment found face to face. It is not at all comfortable to express being a gay man to anyone—not even another gay brotha. Thus for your birthday mom I began to actually fight with more and even more desire. Using the tool of strength together with the power of writing got the thinking about my hopeless situation under real interrogation. Let us go back a number of months to the spring of 1992. A program back home in Seattle came to a shelter I was in to recruit those interested in working their way out of homelessness, addiction and the many other factors of life that finds end results in places like the shelter I had to try and dwell in. This shelter was located in Seattle's Pioneer Square, the south end of downtown. This foundation offered employment under their program guidelines for a one year time period. Pay raises would come during this program's progress. A team of counselors, the director, assistant director, team coordinators and what was indeed a solid program geared to enhance that decision to get it together made by the program participant/client generally made up this program. I applied for and achieved entrance into this program. Pay began at $5.15 per hour. I was able to get a very cheap apartment in the Yesler Terrace ghetto in my home. I worked on a couple of the teams until my epilepsy changed my goals in the field with other team members to the office and reception area of this program located at that time on Elliott Avenue. I trained in the office as a receptionist. I also trained in other office knowledge and procedures. I'll never forget Suzie J. I know she won't forget me as I did a portrait of her favorite TV personality who was a great idol of hers. But I continued to get high. The program was indeed aware of this and is when and where the counselors went to work with mentoring and counseling tactics used to get my mind and other fighting abilities to actually fight back the addict in me. They would take my money and pay my rent and other living expenses. I would have to ask for and give reason for money I did indeed achieve from my counselor. I'll never forget you Jan. You indeed made sure I got to a point with myself to do or die—my own choice. And it took five months to get to this stage. Thus the writing that began on July 29th, 1992 is the real war that began on September 19th of that year. The day before a rainy Saturday morning I had again found enough money through lies to Jan and whatever else to continue an affair with a brotha I knew out of prison. It was very early in the morning around 4AM when for some strange reason I simply took the plate of dope we were smoking, walked to the bathroom and flushed it!! Saturday was a day of overtime for anyone wanting to make that money. John was shocked but said nothing due to both our, of course, paranoid condition from all the smoking. Sex had again been a burnt out camel cigarette smoked for over twenty years. I said nothing accept to ask John to take me to work. I got there pretty early. Upon departing John's car I just looked at him. I knew he could see the message of "no more". I entered the Corps for work. It was easily seen the mysterious and as well humble look on my face. Folks like Bill and Tee knew what was up with me. I didn't even know I was finally in the beginning stages of 100 percent!!! Those at the Corps got busy and put me with whom I term today as the two Angles sent from our Higher Power who took me to the surrendering grounds. I was put on a team with Becky and Tee who both claimed over twenty months into recovery. The Corps was installing water saving shower heads in the city and we were to be stationed in West Seattle. In route to this destination I blurted out one question igniting that whole day of September 19, 1992. "So; what is it about this first step anyway; huh?" Tee simply looked at me with the very stern look he can indeed emit and stated point blank how it was; "I had to find such out. That all he could do was support me in my desires for a positive life". The sea opened up so intensely and so suddenly until all I can vividly recall from this point on is Tee and Becky stopping at an elementary school. Tee got me out of the truck and sat me on the steps in the misty rain of Seattle where I opened up the conversation of surrender to our Higher Power. From this point on I can only recall bits and pieces of this morning of September 19th, 1992. I recall Tee pacing back and forth keeping any Saturday morning kids and any others from mocking or interrupting God's work. I recall seeing Becky sitting in the truck with tears in her eyes as well as seeing Tee with tears as well but a protective kind of glow about him. I recall bits of my begging and pleading as well as expressing mother's death, my sexuality and the continuous tears I could not stop for all of that morning and in fact that entire day. I recall easing up enough for the three of us to simply go back to SCC's headquarters and my being sent home. I remember very well upon arriving at the apartment I had been so actively addicted in how utterly frightened I became—especially when I touched to door knob. It was getting toward the evening hours and daylight saving time was letting go of its many daylight hours for another year. But I did in fact go in the apartment I dwelled in as an addict only to find myself walking with a blanket of sorts wrapped around me in route through Seattle University to a fellowship hall I had visited and attended meetings in the not so recent past. It was not far away from the hell I suffered. I sat there. No one said anything to me or offered any help. It seemed I could hear in the quiet kind of mist someone saying "let him alone; God's got him". And when the first of two meetings were announced I knew immediately why I was sent there. In the first meeting I continued the tears. Moaning began to take full effect. I rocked back and forth as if almost out of control. The second meeting was decided by those of the hall to be a candle light meeting. More crying, moaning, rocking and admitting my desires to become free of the nightmare I knew I lived in followed through this meeting as well. After the meeting was over it was the end of another day at the hall and it began closing down. I said nothing to no one. I simply made the same trail, not far from my apartment, again through Seattle University back home in the light Seattle rain. As soon as I got in the door without any fear whatsoever, I laid my body down. Instant sleep took its course. I woke the next day without any urges or cravings for drugs or sex. The sun had not finished with Seattle as summer was almost over with fall being in the air. The sun was beaming through the window of my apartment upon my waking. All I could do or think about was cleaning this nasty apartment I had lived in for some months now. Old fashion comet, rags and other cleaning materials found me cleaning like mother use to do and get us involved in. Therefore I knew what it was I was after in that apartment, all day, the day after my surrendering and being given not another but this time a real chance at life. What lay ahead after this most important day in my life can indeed and finally be read as footwork—the formation of a solid foundation to build on—that 100 percent needed to finally get a real and especially a positive change in motion. I began communicating with our Higher Power by waking each day with the Serenity Prayer, thanking Him for another day clean and sober and having added that he help us all with His love. If God is indeed a man, white, black or indifferent I do not know. I only know what I felt and experienced the day I was given a real chance to rid my life of addiction. Naming this entity in us all as God being a man is or seems a kind of tradition. Reading the bible and becoming a religious man belonging to a church does not find peace for my life. I instead was led by something inside me to freedom. Good and bad feelings that I get were and continue to be for my best interest. I know life will be no easy piece of cake from this point on—hence again and this time **REAL** footwork. But the challenge was accepted the day I surrendered and I want to see what if any success I can still make of my life. Can I at least put these thoughts and feelings in written form for others to endure for their own sake and knowledge of such an evil part of life? I ain't nobody different than the basic language of addiction when it comes to having had enough and knowing it by the frightened condition continuing to grow. Getting to this point is for those others to heed and find in their own unique ways—ways because there are many.